T0277473

Botanical Cocktails

Botanical Cocktails

50 GARDEN-TO-GLASS BEVERAGES FOR EVERY SEASON

TENAE STEWART, AUTHOR OF
THE MODERN WITCH'S GUIDE TO NATURAL MAGICK

Skyhorse Publishing

Skyhorse Publishing books may be purchased in bulk at special discounts for sales promotion, corporate gifts, fund-raising, or educational purposes. Special editions can also be created to specifications. For details, contact the Special Sales Department, Skyhorse Publishing, 307 West 36th Street, 11th Floor, New York, NY 10018 or info@skyhorsepublishing.com.

Skyhorse® and Skyhorse Publishing® are registered trademarks of Skyhorse Publishing, Inc.®, a Delaware corporation.

Visit our website at www.skyhorsepublishing.com.

10 9 8 7 6 5 4 3 2 1

Library of Congress Cataloging-in-Publication Data is available on file.

Cover design by Kai Texel
Cover photos by Jade Hincks

Print ISBN: 978-1-5107-7812-2
Ebook ISBN: 978-1-5107-7813-9

Printed in China

Contents

Chapter 1: AN INTRODUCTION TO BOTANICAL COCKTAILS   1

Chapter 2: MIXING ELIXIRS   10

Chapter 3: PLANTS & HERBS FOR THE BAR CART   23

Chapter 4: SPRING COCKTAILS & MOCKTAILS   41

Chapter 5: SUMMER COCKTAILS & MOCKTAILS   60

Chapter 6: AUTUMN COCKTAILS & MOCKTAILS   79

Chapter 7: WINTER COCKTAILS & MOCKTAILS   100

Appendix   119

    RECIPES BY SEASON   120

    RECIPES BY PLANT   123

    RECIPES BY ALCOHOL   133

Metric Conversions   137

CHAPTER 1

An Introduction to Botanical Cocktails

Welcome to the world of botanical cocktails! Of course, all cocktails are botanical in some ways, as most forms of alcohol come from some type of plant: grains, fruits, berries, and more. But you can also introduce fresh herbs, flowers, fruits, and botanical liqueurs into your cocktail experience to align your celebrations intentionally with the earth and with nature!

In this book, we're going to explore how to mix your own cocktails using botanical ingredients, where to source and how to grow your own ingredients, and how to work intentionally with plants to create cocktails that embody joy and abundance in every season.

I write and teach about a lot of self-care practices and the one thing they all have in common is that they support us in living our most magical lives. A well-rounded self-care practice nourishes your mind and mental health, cares for your physical body, nurtures your intuition and self-trust, and makes you feel connected to something larger than yourself— the earth, your community, and more.

Doesn't that sound magical? Nature is a powerful ally in creating a life that is whimsical and full of celebration. Throughout the changing tides of the seasons, we experience celebrations of all kinds. There are holidays, birthdays, and small, everyday moments that naturally align with the earth, be it a summer afternoon on the patio with friends or a family visit to the pumpkin patch.

These rhythms are not just marked by commercial holidays but also by our natural desire to bring light to the darkness of winter and enjoy the summer sunshine while it lasts. Honoring these rhythms with our awareness, gratitude, and festivity is a powerful form of self-care, because it helps us stay in tune with ourselves.

But can we really go so far as to say *cocktails* are a form of self-care, just because they're made with plants? In some ways, absolutely!

For one thing, every recipe in this book is paired with a nonalcoholic "mocktail" variation, as the festive atmosphere and people around should be the only necessary ingredients in any celebration. But whether we take alcohol out of the equation, mixing botanical beverages for all your seasonal celebrations, big and small, has many benefits. The very act of creating a special beverage for you and your loved ones to enjoy can be a ritual in and of itself. From harvesting or selecting the ingredients, chopping and dicing, muddling them together, to that first delicious sip, all the steps in this process can be done with care and intention.

Working with plants directly from the earth is a powerful opportunity to reconnect with nature. Whether you commune with plants by working in the garden, hiking and foraging, making teas and tinctures, or by mixing up some fun and festive cocktails, this direct connection to nature's wisdom is more accessible than we may realize in today's world.

Any opportunity to connect with the earth can be healing and a way to nourish ourselves. No, cocktails don't have the nutritional or immune-boosting value that you would find by practicing traditional herbalism, but there is also healing to be found in embracing joy and pleasure—you could argue that is our purpose here, so if a botanical cocktail or mocktail can help you brew up a little fun *and* connect with the earth, that definitely sounds like self-care to me!

HOW TO ALIGN YOUR CELEBRATIONS WITH NATURE

Working with the wisdom of plants and the seasons is also powerful self-care. Whether you grow them yourself or purchase them at the grocery store or farmers' market, plants carry a powerful energetic signature. They can be soothing, uplifting, joyful, or comforting. These qualities might come from your own associations with the scent or flavor of a plant, such as the warm, comforting scent of cinnamon cookies baking in the oven when you were a child. Other times, these qualities might come from the physiological impact a plant has on our nervous system, such as how lavender and chamomile are known to soothe and relax the mind.

Just as often, these qualities come from the ancient associations of plants with gods, goddesses, and planets. Lemons have long been associated with the moon and lunar goddesses, while oranges have often been linked to the sun and are said to bring joy and happiness. Pomegranates are connected to the underworld myths of Persephone, so they are associated with transformation, while roses are long held to be sacred to the love goddess, Venus.

When you work with plants in the form of herbalism, whether mixing teas and tinctures (or, yes, even cocktails!), you invite all of this personal and ancient history into your life. When you make those selections intentionally, you can call in the emotions and experiences you wish to embody.

Want more love or self-love in your life? A rose and berry concoction may be in order, such as the Tastes Like Pink Sangria (Berry Rose Sangria) on page 64. Want more joy and happiness? An orange and clove libation could be just the thing, like the Brandy Orange Blossom (Orange Pomander) on page 105.

There's also a very important seasonal component here. Just as fruits and veggies taste more delicious and full-bodied when they are in season, plants are also at their most energetically potent when they are fresh and in-season (or aligned with the energy of the current season, which is not always the same thing).

For example, roses are most potent in the spring and summer, when they are in full bloom. We can rely on dried roses or rose water at other times of the year, but we tend to feel most called to the supportive and loving energy of rose when we are in spring or summer. Then again, if you're feeling down on a particularly gray winter day, you might use rose water to perk up your spirits and call in a bit of summer sunshine! Which plant allies you feel drawn to at certain times is a very intuitive process, so trust your gut on what you are craving.

The same goes for what types of cocktails you want to mix up at different times of the year. Margaritas and mojitos tend to be most popular in the summer, while hot toddies and mulled wine are most commonly enjoyed in the winter. This isn't just about cold drinks when it's hot and vice versa—it's also about the flavor profiles and energy of the plants involved.

For example, summertime is all about heat—literally and figuratively. Spices like cayenne and tajin can help you channel that fiery energy, while abundant, in-season herbs like mint and thyme offer much-needed cooling and grounding. In the wintertime, we're drawn to in-season citrus and bright spices, which help enliven the darkest days.

In many ways, botanical cocktails are an invitation to practice mindfulness and seasonal intentionality. Spring is the season of the air element, all about fresh starts, rebirth, and new beginnings. Plants that are energetically aligned with spring are those that are light, fresh, and fragrant. Summer is the season of the fire element, all about joy, celebration, and taking action. Plants that are energetically aligned with summer are those that are in full fruit or full bloom and those that have some heat to them. Autumn is the season of the water element, all about getting in touch with our intuition, honoring the dead, and celebrating abundance. Plants that are energetically aligned with autumn are those that are being harvested and that connect us with our ancestors and intuition. Winter is the season of the earth element, all about rest, retreat, and bringing light to the darkness. Plants that are energetically aligned with winter are those that warm or light us up from within and that soothe our souls with comfort and peace. We'll talk more about specific plants to work with for each season in Chapter 3 (page 23).

MIXING COCKTAILS AS A SEASONAL RITUAL

For the purposes of this book, we're specifically going to talk about how you can mix and enjoy cocktails as a seasonal ritual in celebration of the earth and nature. These principles really apply to any kind of cooking or herbalism where you are choosing ingredients and combining them with love and intention. The idea here is to give your full attention to what you're doing and to put intention into what you're creating. This helps you to both clear your head—think of this like a moving meditation—and create something beautiful and delicious. This is what we mean when we say something is "made with love!"

Anything can be meditative, so long as we do it mindfully. I like to talk about brewing a cup of tea as a beautiful form of meditation. We select the ingredients, prepare the pot of tea, watch the color of the herbs unfurl in the water as it steeps, and savor the first sip. Tea rituals like this can be found in cultures all across the world, but this mindful, meditative experience isn't limited to making a cup of tea! We can practice a very similar ritual of noticing the scents, sounds, flavors, and colors of nature as we work to create the delicious drinks in this book.

The earth provides so much abundance for us to enjoy and consume, but this is not a one-sided relationship. For one thing, Mother Nature can take away just as readily as she can provide. But we also have to do our part to give back to the earth, to ask permission for what we wish to use, and to give thanks and gratitude for what we take. I highly recommend growing your own ingredients for botanical cocktails or gathering them from your local farmers' market, when possible, as this closer connection to the earth will make your plant allies not only taste better but be more energetically potent as well!

MINDFUL BLENDING RITUAL

You can apply this practice to any of the cocktails in this book or any other recipe that you enjoy making!

1. Choose your ingredients and arrange them on the cutting board in front of you.
2. Take a moment to inhale the scent of the fresh herbs, fruits, or flowers you've chosen. Close your eyes and really savor their freshness.
3. Go about chopping, dicing, or any other preparations that are needed, keeping your mind focused on the task at hand and on the ways that these ingredients represent and embody the energy of the current season.
4. Begin mixing the ingredients together per the recipe, paying careful attention to how the fresh ingredients bring color to the liquids, the sound of ice clinking, and any other sensory elements.
5. As you mix, focus on how you intend for yourself and anyone else enjoying this beverage to feel while they drink it. Pour your desired feelings of love, joy, abundance, gratitude, calm, or relaxation into your actions. You might even speak your intentions aloud as you work.
6. When you are ready, pour yourself a glass and take that first sip, giving your complete attention to the flavor and scent of the beverage, provided in part by your plant allies, and on the intentions you have set.

CHAPTER 2

Mixing Elixirs

Making your own botanical cocktails at home doesn't have to be difficult! You'll want to stock your home bar with a few essentials and familiarize yourself with some classic cocktails to use as inspiration.

In this chapter, we're going to get into all the nitty gritty details of having your own botanical bar at home! First, we'll cover the main types of alcohol included in the recipes in this book and some of the classic cocktails they feature in. Then, we'll go over the mixers, garnishes, and other ingredients to have on hand and finally, we'll cover the tools and glassware you will want to use.

It's not necessary to fully outfit a bar with everything in this chapter. Rather, I'd start with three or four kinds of alcohol that you prefer, a couple different kinds of glasses and your preferred tools, and adding mixers like bitters and liqueurs as you try out new recipes.

TYPES OF ALCOHOL AND COCKTAIL BASES

Most of the recipes in this book are inspired by classic cocktails. Mixing and matching classic combinations of fruit and alcohol with your

favorite herbs, flowers, and more are great ways to create botanical cocktails.

Gin cocktails are the most readily botanical recipes because gin itself is made with juniper berries and other fruits, herbs, and spices! Traditional gin cocktails are particularly adaptable and diverse, and they form the base of numerous recipes in this book.

The gin fizz is one of the most impressive cocktails you can whip up with its signature layer of foam on top, but it's surprisingly easy to make!

A gin and tonic is just what it says: gin mixed with tonic water and often a bit of lime juice. You'll find that lime juice is a common ingredient in many recipes for the slightly sour tang it adds to other flavors.

One of my favorite gin cocktails is the French 75, which combines gin and sparkling wine, (such as champagne), with a bit of simple syrup or a sugar cube.

In fact, there are many ways to incorporate still and sparkling wine into your cocktails, which make for especially easy and accessible recipes. Wine is most commonly made with grapes, although you'll also find fruit wines and honey wines.

There's the mimosa, of course, which is just sparkling wine with fruit juice. It's traditionally made with orange juice, but mix it up with any juice of your choice! Sangria combines wine with sliced fruits, as well as liqueur and typically either brandy or vodka for a little extra kick and to help the flavors mingle.

A spritz is another great sparkling wine cocktail that's perfect for a warm spring or summer evening and is very popular with vacationers in Italy. It combines prosecco with club soda and traditionally Aperol or the mixers of your choice.

Of course, I'm from California, so you'll find quite a few tequila cocktails in this book as well. There are margaritas, which combine tequila, orange liqueur, and lime juice, and palomas, which mix tequila, lime, and grapefruit juice. Some recipes call for tequila blanco, which is the tequila you're likely most familiar with, while others call for smoky mezcal. Tequila is made from the agave plant.

We have rum cocktails with all three types of rum, made from sugarcane: dark, white, and spiced, each of which lends itself to different flavor profiles and seasons. Dark rum goes beautifully with darker fruits like blackberry and pomegranate. White rum is perfect for your bright, vibrant mojitos, mixed with lime, and spiced rum adds cozy warmth to all your fall favorites like pumpkin punch.

Of course, we can't forget our brandy and whiskey cocktails either. Brandy is a form of distilled wine, while whiskey is made with different types of grains. We've got old fashioneds, the most classic original cocktail, and so easy to put a botanical twist on.

There's the traditional hot toddy, which is simply whiskey mixed with water, lemon juice, and honey, and the enduring mint julep, with bourbon, bitters, and mint leaves. These classics already incorporate so many botanical elements, but you better believe we're going to plant-ify them even more!

Finally, we would be remiss to skip the vodka cocktails. Vodka is traditionally made from grains and potatoes. It pairs well with just about anything you desire, from coffee to violets. But my personal favorite vodka cocktail is the mule, which mixes vodka, lime, and ginger beer, a refreshing beverage to be sure.

There are a few other beverages in here, such as mead, but most of the recipes in this book are centered around gin, tequila, whiskey, rum, vodka, and wine. Your home bar does not have to be wildly extensive to make all of the recipes in this book!

MIXERS AND OTHER INGREDIENTS

The main alcoholic ingredients in each recipe are not the only things you'll need to have on hand, though, for your home bar to be complete. There are a few different categories of mixers to keep in mind, both nonalcoholic ingredients, as well as secondary alcoholic elements like liqueurs.

Liqueurs

Aperol: A bright orange Italian liqueur that is most well-known as a key ingredient in the Aperol spritz, a popular cocktail in the Italian riviera.

Campari: Often confused with Aperol, Campari is a dark red Italian liqueur, also made from herbs and fruits, but with a more bitter flavor.

Crème de violette liqueur: This liqueur is potently floral and was especially popular in the 1800s and early 1900s.

Elderflower liqueur: This is one of my favorite floral liqueurs. It's light and delicate and pairs beautifully with other flowers and herbs.

Kahlúa: This is a delicious rum and coffee liqueur that brings the cozy flavor of a cup of coffee to some of your favorite winter cocktails.

Orange liqueur: Probably the most commonly used liqueur, orange liqueur is also known as triple sec. This liqueur is found in everything from sangria to margaritas for a bit of citrus flavor.

Grand Marnier: A simple triple sec orange liqueur is perfect for most cocktails that call for this ingredient, but when you're looking for something a little more elevated, Grand Marnier steps in, as this orange liqueur is made with cognac.

Peach schnapps: This one is not technically a liqueur, as schnapps is actually a distilled spirit, but it is one of the only ingredients of its kind in this book. Peach schnapps is made from distilled and fermented peaches.

Pear liqueur: This spiced fruit liqueur is nuanced and perfect for mixing into your fall cocktails.

Rose hip liqueur: Although somewhat unusual, this sweet-tart liqueur is a wonderful way to bring the flavors of both citrus and rose into your beverages.

Sweet vermouth: Not technically a liqueur, sweet vermouth is actually a fortified wine that is commonly used as a mixer in cocktails.

Of course, there are many more types of liqueurs than this short list, but these are all you will need for the recipes in this book!

NONALCOHOLIC MIXERS

The vast majority of nonalcoholic mixers used in this book are fruit juices. You can absolutely purchase these at the grocery store, or you could take things one step further and juice your own fruits as well!

Lemon juice and lime juice are two of the most common fruit mixers, as their acidity brings a much-needed brightness to many drinks in all seasons. You'll also find the following juices in our recipes for each season as well:

Spring and summer: Guava juice, grapefruit juice
Autumn and winter: Apple juice, blood orange juice, cranberry juice, grapefruit juice, kale juice, orange juice, pomegranate juice

The other most common nonalcoholic mixer is simple syrup, which is a combination of sugar and water, heated until the sugar dissolves. You can purchase premade, unflavored simple syrup, but many of the recipes in this book call for specialty simple syrups. All of them start with this basic recipe:

BASIC SIMPLE SYRUP RECIPE

- 1 cup water
- 1 cup white sugar

1. Combine water and sugar in a saucepan over medium heat.
2. Bring to a boil.
3. Stir until sugar has dissolved.
4. Remove from heat and allow to cool.

Simple syrup is a great way to introduce botanicals into your cocktails, as it can be easily infused with just about any flavor. In this book, we have recipes that call for everything from rosemary simple syrup to lavender simple syrup and even sumac simple syrup! Refer back to this basic recipe to adapt for these infusions.

A few recipes in this book also call for other nonalcoholic mixers so here are a few you may want to have on hand for when the need arises:

- **Agave nectar:** A honey-like substance made from the agave plant that is a wonderful sweetener.
- **Bitters (often ANGOSTURA®):** A common cocktail flavoring, bitters are small bottles of spirits flavored with botanicals. One of the most common is ANGOSTURA® bitters, which are flavored with a secret blend of over forty herbs and spices.
- **Chai spices:** Several recipes in our autumn and winter chapters (pages 79–117) call for chai spices or brewed chai. This is a blend of spices, usually including some combination of cinnamon, clove,

cardamom, star anise, and/or peppercorns. It's very easy to make and adapt to your own taste.

- **Club soda:** An effervescent addition to many beverages that's often used as a topper so it doesn't lose its fizz.
- **Ginger beer:** This refreshing beverage is nonalcoholic, despite the name, and is a classic mixer for mules but adds fizz and kick to many other cocktails as well.
- **Grenadine:** A sweet syrup made from pomegranates and recognizable by its vivid dark red color.
- **Honey:** Although most of our recipes call for simple syrup as a sweetener, made with white sugar, honey is an excellent substitute as well.
- **Orange blossom water:** This potently flavored yet delicate ingredient is made by infusing the flowers of the bitter orange tree in water, also called neroli.
- **Plant-based milks:** Some of our cozier recipes call for or would be complemented by plant-based milks such as oat milk or almond milk.
- **Rose water:** A hydrosol made from the water distillation of rose blossoms; this ingredient is intensely floral.
- **Sparkling water:** The key difference between sparkling water and club soda is that the carbonation in sparkling water occurs naturally, derived from natural springs, while club soda is manufactured.
- **Tonic water:** This ingredient is similar in many ways to club soda, but with the addition of quinine.

GARNISHES

Garnishes are not a necessary part of the cocktail-making process, but they add so much fun, charm, and aesthetic value! A common garnish is simply a bit of fresh fruit from the fruit already included in the recipe, such as a lime wedge, slice of grapefruit, or fresh blackberries. I also like to garnish floral and herbal cocktails with a bit of dried or fresh botanical material, such as dried rosebuds or fresh thyme sprigs.

Another way to garnish your cocktails is with a sugar or salt rim. Salt rims are popular with tequila cocktails like margaritas and palomas. I like to use either flaky sea salt or pink Himalayan salt. Sugar rims are delicious with everything from sangria to sidecars and can be made with both white and brown sugars.

To make a salt or sugar rim, simply place your ingredients on a low, shallow plate. Wet the rim of the glass with a lemon or lime wedge or just a bit of water, then dip the glass upside down in the salt or sugar until it is sufficiently coated. Keep it simple or dress up your rim even more with added citrus zest, ground spices, or other ingredients!

TOOLS

There are a few tools that you'll definitely want to have stocked in your home bar to make mixing up your favorite seasonal elixirs that much easier.

A shaker is a must, with a tightly sealed lid and a strainer component. Many of the cocktails we'll be making together are shaken with ice to combine and chill the ingredients before being strained into a glass.

It will also be convenient to have a jigger or shot glass to measure ingredients in cocktails. Most recipes call for ½ ounce to 3 ounces of each ingredient. A full jigger is 1½ ounces, as are most standard shot glasses, so these are both easy ways to measure.

You may also want a muddler, which is a bar tool for mixing and smashing ingredients together, such as citrus wedges, fresh fruit, and fresh herbs, although I find the back of a wooden spoon works just as well.

Last, a few of our recipes call for ingredients to be blended so a blender or food processor will be useful!

GLASSWARE

You really don't need a lot of fancy glassware to make gorgeous cocktails, although I was very grateful to my grandma for the loan of her beautiful colored glassware collection for the stunning photographs in this book!

In general, most drinks can be made in a rocks glass, which is simply a short glass tumbler, if nothing else is available. If you really want to stock your home bar to the hilt, though, here are the different types of glassware I recommend:

Champagne flute: These tall, shapely glasses are lovely for sipping champagne or mimosas, and I sometimes like to use them for spritzes as well.

Copper mug: These metallic mugs are typically used for mules but are also a stylish choice for punch or mulled wine.

Coupe glass: The original champagne glass, and the ultimate in classy cocktail glassware, this glass is rumored to have been modeled on Marie Antoinette's left breast.

Highball glass: A tall, narrow glass tumbler.

Martini glass: Similar to a coupe glass, martini glasses are tall with a slender stem but with steep, flat sides instead of curved ones.

Rocks glass: A short glass tumbler, ideal for old fashioneds and margaritas on the rocks.

Wine glass or goblet: Whether you prefer stemmed or stemless glasses, wine glasses or goblets make for an excellent glassware option for many cocktails.

You're now an expert in mixing and matching ingredients and glassware for your botanical cocktails! In the next chapter, we'll explore more about the process of working with plants in your cocktail adventures.

CHAPTER 3

Plants & Herbs for the Bar Cart

Plants are at the core of all cocktail books, even if they're not as explicit about it as this one. As we learned in the last chapter, vodka is made from potatoes, gin is made from juniper berries, wine from grapes, and whiskey from grains, so even the simplest glass of wine or most low-key bar order has a connection to the natural world. In this chapter, we're taking it to the next level and exploring the role that whole plants, herbs, flowers, fruits, and spices can play in your cocktails.

First: Why would you want to incorporate plants into your bar cart essentials? Aren't liquors, liqueurs, and bitters plenty?

When you combine your favorite beverages with gifts from the earth, they can help call in more of what you desire in your life. Every plant carries a particular energetic signature, influenced by its color, flavor, season, and even by the planets. Working with the energy of a plant that is in season or that aligns with a seasonal energy you wish to embody in your life is a beautiful way to celebrate joyfully.

WHERE TO SOURCE INGREDIENTS

It's very important that the ingredients you use in your cocktails are edible, preferably organic, and always toxin-free. Local and fresh herbs, fruits, and spices can be easily acquired at your local grocery store or farmers' market, in many cases. Be sure to wash anything you purchase, just as you would before cooking a meal.

You should not buy flowers from a flower shop to use in your cocktails unless the florist can guarantee that the flowers are safe to eat and grown on a local, organic farm. Flowers that are imported or grown on nonorganic farms are often sprayed with inedible pesticides which can be okay for floral arrangements, but not so much for human consumption!

In some cases, you may be able to forage for some of your ingredients, meaning that you collect them directly from where they grow wild in nature. There are a few very important things to consider when foraging:

1. Only harvest plants if you are completely certain you know what they are. Some poisonous and toxic plants bear very similar resemblance to common ingredients so it's essential that you know what you are harvesting.
2. Always take just what you need, never more. This allows the plants to replenish themselves and continue producing.
3. Do not harvest from the side of the road, as fumes from vehicles can be highly toxic and can cling to plants.
4. Clean and dry foraged ingredients thoroughly.
5. Only harvest from locations that you have safe and legal access to.

The most important thing to consider when foraging is your own confidence level. If you aren't certain what a plant is, don't harvest and consume it! I also recommend taking classes and reading books about foraging to strengthen your knowledge in this area before consuming plants you find.

HOW TO GROW YOUR OWN INGREDIENTS

Of course, the most sustainable and potent way to source botanical ingredients is to grow them yourself! You can grow herbs and flowers whether you have a big backyard garden or small windowsill or balcony.

I recommend starting with five to eight plants in small pots, especially if you are new to growing your own herbs. Choose a few herbs that will be versatile for lots of different botanical cocktail recipes, or even for cooking and other purposes as well. Some good basic herbs include mint, sage, rosemary, and thyme, as these are all very easy to grow. *One word of caution is that if you plant mint, be sure to give it its own pot and never put it directly in the ground, because it can take over an entire space very quickly!*

You might also choose a few flowers to grow yourself. Some good basic flowers to start with include lavender and rose. These will both do okay in pots, although they tend to grow better directly in the ground if possible.

With both herbs and flowers, I like to harvest in the summer and early fall (your harvest date will depend on your own location and climate), then bundle the cut ingredients and hang them to dry in a window. This gives you homegrown dried ingredients to work with throughout the fall and winter months! You can even grow some herbs inside in windowsill pots during the winter to have fresh ingredients year-round.

You can also grow your own fruits, although this is a more advanced option! Berry bushes are easier to grow (though be aware that they can spread quickly), and small citrus and fruit trees are often perfectly happy in large pots.

Do a little bit of research on whether the plants you've chosen prefer full or partial sun so that you can place them in as ideal a location as possible. I like to sprinkle organic fertilizer around the base of my herbs and citrus plants every six to eight weeks to help them grow to their fullest potential.

Aside from sustainability and the delicious flavor of fresh, homegrown ingredients, another perk of growing your own plants is working with them from seed (or starter), all the way to the glass.

PLANT PROFILES

The rest of this chapter includes profiles of some common plants to elevate your cocktail-making experience! Of course, these are just a handful of the plants you can use to make botanical cocktails and even just a few of those you'll find in this book, but these sixteen plant allies represent and embody each of the seasons.

First, we're going to start with profiles of a few common herbs (plants with leaves or flowers that are often used for flavoring and medicinal purposes).

Thyme

There are myriad herbs available in spring and summer. To start us off, I've chosen thyme as our spring herb because it has a light and aromatic flavor that pairs well with spring fruits and citrus. You'll find thyme represented in a few different spring and summer recipes in this book, paired with everything from grapefruit, peach, and blackberries to rum and sparkling wine. Thyme is a wonderful ally to work with when you want an earthiness and a grounded energy that still feels light and airy.

Latin Name: *Thymus vulgaris*

Folk Names: Garden thyme, farigoule

In Season: Late spring and summer

Parts of Plant Used: Leaves

Zodiac Connections: Mercury, Virgo

Healing Properties: Antibacterial, relieves cough, may improve hair growth and memory

Folklore Uses: Promotes good health, psychic ability, and courage

Precautions: Might slow blood clotting

Sage

Sage is a wonderful summer herb that carries us into fall. It's often found in savory fall dishes, but it can add a layer of herbaceous dimension and depth to your favorite cocktails as well. You'll find sage represented in a few different ways in our summer and fall recipes, paired with sweet honey, smoky flavors, apple, lime, and more. Sage is most commonly used as a plant ally for purification and cleansing. It's often burned as incense or for smoke cleansing, but it's clearing qualities and wise nature can be cultivated in other ways as well.

Latin Name: *Salvia officinalis*

Folk Names: Garden sage, sawge

In Season: Midsummer

Parts of Plant Used: Leaves

Zodiac Connections: Jupiter, Sagittarius

Healing Properties: Improves clarity and memory, supports high cholesterol

Folklore Uses: Purifies negative energy, promotes wisdom and immortality

Precautions: Possibly unsafe for people who are pregnant or breastfeeding

Rosemary

Another herb that takes us easily from summer into fall is rosemary, although I find myself turning to this plant ally most in autumn. Like sage, it pairs well with smoky, earthy, and savory flavors and brings a more grounded energy to all of the above. In our autumn recipe chapter (page 79), you'll find rosemary paired with citrus, spices, pomegranates, and more. Rosemary is commonly associated with tradition, legacy, and

remembering the past, which makes it a fine fit for our fall herb. As Ophelia said: "Rosemary for remembrance . . ."

Latin Name: *Salvia rosmarinus*
Folk Names: Elf leaf, compass weed
In Season: Summer into fall
Parts of Plant Used: Leaves
Zodiac Connections: Sun, Saturn, Capricorn
Healing Properties: Anti-inflammatory, may improve memory
Folklore Uses: Promotes protection of people and spaces, improves mental functions, banishes negativity
Precautions: None

Peppermint

Although peppermint is in season primarily in the summer months, it is often associated with winter. The cool, refreshing flavor of mint is reminiscent of the colder part of the year, so I've chosen it as our winter herb here.

Latin Name: *Mentha piperita*
Folk Names: Lament, brandy mint
In Season: Spring into fall
Parts of Plant Used: Leaves
Zodiac Connections: Mercury, Gemini
Healing Properties: Supports stomach pain and indigestion
Folklore Uses: Promotes love, healing, and purification
Precautions: None

Flowers are also wonderful ingredients to use in your botanical cocktails.

So many flowers are edible, and they bring a lovely scent, color, and flavor to mixed drinks.

Lavender

Lavender is one of my absolute favorite herbs, and the flowers are primarily used (as opposed to the leaves of the herb, which are more commonly used in herbalism practices). This heavenly scented flower makes a perfect pairing with lemon, rose, berries, and more. In our spring and summer chapters (pages 41–78), you'll find a number of light and bright recipes incorporating fresh lavender. Though it's best known for its beautiful color and scent, lavender also has a delicious and distinct flavor that's perfect for spring.

Latin Name: *Lavandula angustifolia*

Folk Names: Nardus, spike

In Season: Late spring to late summer

Parts of Plant Used: Flowers

Zodiac Connections: Mercury, Gemini, Pisces

Healing Properties: Relieves anxiety, promotes calm and peaceful sleep

Folklore Uses: Promotes psychic dreams, encourages love

Precautions: None

Rose

Rose is one of my favorite flowers to work with in herbalism because it's so versatile. In fact, you'll find rose used in multiple recipes throughout this book! We are most likely to use rose petals in summer when they are freshest but you might incorporate rose water, rose hips, or rose simple

syrup any time of year to harness the delicate flavor and loving energy of this beautiful plant ally.

Latin Name: *Rosa centifolia*

Folk Names: Provence rose

In Season: Late spring to early fall

Parts of Plant Used: Flowers, Fruit

Zodiac Connections: Venus, Taurus, Libra

Healing Properties: Fruit (rose hip) supports immune system and reduces pain and stiffness; petals support grief and stomachaches

Folklore Uses: Used for divination to find one's true love, promotes healing, love, and good fortune

Precautions: None

Elderflower

Even though elderflower is actually in season in early summer, I often find myself using dried elderflower and elderflower liqueur in autumn, either alongside elderberry (the berries of the same tree) or paired with other gentle flavors like honey. It's a wonderful transitional flower to carry some of the softer, gentler energy of spring and summer into the moodier days of fall.

Latin Name: *Sambucus nigra*

Folk Names: Eldrun, witches' tree

In Season: Early summer

Parts of Plant Used: Flowers (also the berries of the same tree)

Zodiac Connections: Venus, Libra

Healing Properties: Anti-inflammatory, supports immune system

Folklore Uses: Banishes negativity, promotes prosperity and magical support

Precautions: The raw, uncooked flowers are mildly toxic

Hibiscus

There are very few flowers that bloom in the winter months and even fewer that are edible. However, that makes winter a great time to work with tropical flowers like hibiscus that call in the loving energy of summer and warmer days! Hibiscus is a stunningly beautiful flower and its dried petals bring vibrant color to any beverage. It has a tart flavor that pairs well with sweet and spicy ingredients and you can't beat the color for winter holiday treats.

Latin Name: *Hibiscus rosa-sinensis*

Folk Names: Sorrel, rose of sharon

In Season: Late summer into fall

Parts of Plant Used: Flowers

Zodiac Connections: Venus, Taurus, Libra

Healing Properties: May help lower high blood pressure and cholesterol

Folklore Uses: Used as an aphrodisiac, promotes love and sensuality

Precautions: Can cause blood pressure to drop

Although we don't always see them growing in their natural environment, our favorite spices also come from plants! Spices are often made from the bark or seeds of trees and other plants.

Ginger

You'll find ginger in recipes scattered throughout this book, especially in the form of ginger beer which is an excellent nonalcoholic mixer, but I love ginger for spring because it has a bright, lively bite to it that really wakes you up. Ginger is great for cutting the sweetness of fresh fruits and for adding a note of spiciness to floral and herbal flavors as well.

Latin Name: *Zingiber offinale*

Folk Names: Canton, singabera

In Season: Fall into winter

Parts of Plant Used: Rhizomes

Zodiac Connections: Mars, Aries

Healing Properties: Relieves nausea, vomiting, and menstrual cramps

Folklore Uses: Boosts power and success, calls in money

Precautions: Can cause heartburn and skin irritation

Chili Pepper

You won't find chili pepper in very many cocktail recipes but it's an excellent spice to kick things up a notch. Whether working with whole peppers or the spicy seeds, chili pepper embodies the hot, hot, hot energy of summer! It's best used sparingly, such as in a salt rim, but you might experiment with adding it to some of your favorite fruity summer drinks for something a little more bold.

Latin Name: *Capsicum annuum*

Folk Names: Canton, gingifra

In Season: Summer

Parts of Plant Used: Fruit, seeds

Zodiac Connections: Mars, Aries

Healing Properties: Supports chronic pain and nerve damage

Folklore Uses: Promotes fidelity in relationships, breaks bad luck or curses

Precautions: Can cause skin and stomach irritation

Cinnamon

Cinnamon is the ultimate fall spice, often found in baked goods, pumpkin spice lattes, and cocktails of all kinds. Many recipes that include cinnamon in this book feature it as one of the many chai spices, a unique and flavorful spice blend that's well-suited to other fall ingredients like apple and pomegranate. Even just a cinnamon stick added to a fall cocktail as garnish lends warmth, flavor, and coziness.

Latin Name: *Cinnamomum verum*

Folk Names: Canella, sweet wood

In Season: Harvested in summer and fall

Parts of Plant Used: Bark

Zodiac Connections: Sun, Leo

Healing Properties: Anti-inflammatory, helps control blood sugar

Folklore Uses: Promotes success, protects people and places, encourages love and passion

Precautions: Can cause skin irritation

Clove

Though slightly more divisive than cinnamon, clove is another of the classic fall spices often found in chai blends. Clove has a bittersweet quality that's earthy and more unusual than that of cinnamon. Although it's often called a fall spice, I love clove especially in the winter when its unique flavors really shine. Whole cloves sprinkled into a simmering pot of mulled wine or apple cider always conjure up holiday memories.

Latin Name: *Syzygium aromaticum*

Folk Names: Carenfil

In Season: Harvested in fall and early spring

Parts of Plant Used: Flower buds

Zodiac Connections: Jupiter, Sagittarius

Healing Properties: May relieve pain, especially from toothaches and indigestion

Folklore Uses: Protects homes and purifies negative energy

Precautions: Might lower blood sugar levels

And of course, we find whole fruits and fruit juices in most cocktail recipes as well. These give us the vibrant colors and delicious flavors that are signature to botanical cocktails throughout the seasons.

Grapefruit

Grapefruits find their way into many different cocktail recipes, as they're the perfect balance of sweet and tart and not as sour as other citrus juices and fruits. A grapefruit is actually a cross between a pomelo and an orange. They're in season in winter, like most citrus, but they remain easy to find fresh into the early spring months, and grapefruit juice is available year-round. It pairs beautifully with herbs, spices, and other fruits, adapting to any mood.

Latin Name: *Citrus paradisi*

Folk Names: Pomelo, pink grapefruit

In Season: Winter into early spring

Parts of Plant Used: Fruit, rind

Zodiac Connections: Moon, Cancer

Healing Properties: May support high cholesterol and immune system

Folklore Uses: Cleanses the energetic aura, purifies negativity, promotes love

Precautions: Interacts with many prescription medications; check with your doctor if it is safe for you to have

Strawberry

Strawberries are the peak of summer perfection. If you've ever had the opportunity to pick fresh, red, juicy strawberries and enjoy them straight from the vine, then you know what I mean. Early summer is characterized by these ubiquitous berries in full fruit. Strawberry pairs naturally with rhubarb and other berries like blueberries and blackberries throughout spring and summer. It makes for a particularly fruity cocktail, but floral and more bitter components can cut the sweet and elevate strawberries for any occasion.

Latin Name: *Fragaria ananassa*

Folk Names: Streawberge, strewberry

In Season: Spring and summer

Parts of Plant Used: Fruit

Zodiac Connections: Venus, Taurus

Healing Properties: May support high cholesterol, heart disease, and diabetes

Folklore Uses: Promotes good luck, encourages love

Precautions: None

Apple

Apples are as magical and full of wisdom as they are healthy and delicious. These plant allies have been revered by many different cultures for millennia and have many health benefits. But they're perfectly yummy in your favorite fall cocktails, too! Apple is used throughout this book's fall and winter recipes in numerous ways, including apple juice, apple cider, hard cider, sliced apples, and more. Apple pairs wonderfully with both spices and herbal notes in a variety of cocktails.

Latin Name: *Malus pumila*

Folk Names: Fruit of the underworld, silver branch

In Season: Late summer into fall

Parts of Plant Used: Fruit

Zodiac Connections: Venus, Libra

Healing Properties: Anti-inflammatory and antibacterial

Folklore Uses: Promotes love and healing, associated with immortality and wisdom

Precautions: Apple seeds are poisonous

Pomegranate

One of my absolute favorite fruits, especially in the rainy winter months, is pomegranate. Although plucking fresh pomegranate seeds can be a messy job, these glittering jewels are a flavorful and visually stunning addition to recipes of all kinds. I love to pair pomegranate with fall spices and herbs like rosemary, but it's also delicious and nuanced with everything from rose water to lime juice.

Latin Name: *Punica granatum*

Folk Names: Carthage apple, grenadier

In Season: Fall into early winter

Parts of Plant Used: Seeds called arils

Zodiac Connections: Pluto, Scorpio

Healing Properties: Supports high blood pressure

Folklore Uses: Used for divination and magic, grants wishes, encourages fertility and wealth

Precautions: Only the seeds should be eaten, as the root, stem, and peel can be toxic

CHAPTER 4

Spring Cocktails & Mocktails

Spring is the season of fresh starts and new beginnings. Spring brings "new year, new me" vibes, often much more so than January. This is the time of year when we truly set our intentions for the seasons ahead, make plans for the year, and look forward with eager anticipation.

So many festivals and celebrations from around the world celebrate the start of spring as a time of beginning again. Many of these are linked to the spring equinox in some way. The equinox occurs each year in the northern hemisphere around March 20 (and in the southern hemisphere around September 20). This is one of two days a year when day and night are equal and balanced.

Nowruz, the Persian New Year, occurs each year on the spring equinox, as does Ostara, the Celtic and Germanic neo-pagan celebrations of spring. Holi is the Hindu spring celebration, a joyful and vibrant festival of colors that occurs in mid-March. Even Easter, the Christian celebration of the rebirth of Jesus Christ, is calculated based on the spring equinox–it occurs in March or April on the first Sunday after the first full moon after the equinox. Passover, also known as Pesach, is a Jewish holiday that celebrates the Hebrew exodus from Egypt and occurs on one of the first full moons in spring as well.

There are also ancient spring festivals that, while not practiced anymore, offer a fascinating look at how springtime has been celebrated by humanity throughout history. These ancient festivals include the Greek Anthesteria in March, which honors Dionysus (the god of wine), and the Roman Floralia in April, which honors Flora (the goddess of flowers). There was also Navigium Isidis in Egypt in March, a procession that honored Isis, the goddess of motherhood, magic, and royalty.

Later in the spring, we might find ourselves celebrating May Day, also known as Beltane, with flower crowns, frolicking, and a cheerful maypole. Mother's Day celebrations occur in the spring and honor the women and caregivers who nurture us (an apt time of year for it, when Mother Nature is also in full bloom).

Those born under the constellations of Aries, Taurus, and Gemini also celebrate their birthdays in the spring. Those born under Aries are fiery, vibrant folks with a passion for life and a determination to create something new for themselves. Taureans are earthy, sensual individuals with a strong connection to nature and the simple pleasures of life. And Geminis are the social butterflies of the zodiac, inviting lively conversation and cheerful energy everywhere they go.

You might find yourself in need of a refreshing spring cocktail for any of these festive celebrations and we've got you covered with thirteen delicious recipes in this chapter!

> All recipes in this chapter make a single serving, unless otherwise noted.

As Thyme Goes By
GRAPEFRUIT THYME MIMOSA

Citrus of all kinds is at its juiciest and most flavorful in late winter and early spring. As soon as grapefruits hit the produce shelves at my local grocery store at the start of the year, I'm eager to bring them home for a deliciously tart breakfast. But what if we didn't just have grapefruit as a breakfast staple this time of year . . . but also as part of our favorite brunch beverage? This tasty grapefruit mimosa will carry you from New Year's Day right into the first warm days of spring.

- 2 ounces grapefruit juice
- 3 ounces sparkling wine
- Fresh thyme sprig, to garnish

1. Pour grapefruit juice into a champagne flute.
2. Top with sparkling wine.
3. Garnish with a fresh thyme sprig.

MAKE IT A MOCKTAIL

Substitute sparkling wine with sparkling juice or cider.

Warrior Princess

GINGER PALOMA

Ginger provides a wonderful kick to this early spring cocktail that takes advantage of in-season grapefruits. We're making use of the whole grapefruit here, from the juice to the fruit to the zest. The hint of spice and delectable fizz create a balanced beverage that is perfect for those unseasonably warm spring days on the back porch. Add a little agave nectar and pink Himalayan salt to bring out the sweetness of the usually tart grapefruit!

SALT RIM

- Medium coarse pink Himalayan salt
- Grapefruit zest
- Lime wedge

COCKTAIL

- 2 ounces grapefruit juice
- ½ ounce lime juice
- 2 ounces tequila
- Agave nectar, to taste
- 2 ounces ginger beer
- Grapefruit slice, to garnish

1. Mix the salt and grapefruit zest together on a low, shallow plate. Wet the rim of a rocks glass with a lime wedge, then dip the rim in the salt until it's evenly coated.
2. Fill the glass half full with ice.
3. Pour in the grapefruit juice, lime juice, tequila, and agave nectar. Stir.
4. Pour ginger beer over other ingredients.
5. Garnish with a slice of grapefruit.

MAKE IT A MOCKTAIL

Substitute tequila with ginger beer.

Bubbly Personality
SPARKLING LEMONADE

Serves: 6

There's nothing more refreshing on a sunny spring day in the garden than a glass of freshly squeezed lemonade! This sweet-tart treat is made even more delicious by the addition of your favorite sparkling wine. Almost like a particularly vibrant mimosa, a garnish of lavender or rose petals elevates this brunch staple whether you're sipping it at a bridal shower, a fancy birthday bash, or just an average Sunday morning.

- ½ cup simple syrup
- Juice of 6 lemons
- 2 cups water
- 2 cups sparkling wine
- Fresh lavender sprig or rose petals

1. Add the simple syrup and lemon juice to a tall pitcher and stir until syrup has dissolved.
2. Add the water and sparkling wine and stir.
3. Refrigerate and serve chilled.
4. Garnish with a sprig of lavender or rose petals.

MAKE IT A MOCKTAIL

Substitute sparkling wine with sparkling water or club soda.

The Front Porch
LAVENDER LEMON SPRITZ

Just as spring starts to turn to summer, the lavender bushes are suddenly in full bloom, their delicate and distinctive fragrance filling the air. Lavender pairs beautifully with lemon, the floral and citrus notes complementing one another in everything from scones to your new favorite beverage, this lavender lemon spritz. Prosecco and club soda add an effervescent note, perfect for sipping on the front porch or a blanket at the park.

- 2 ounces lemon juice (or limoncello)
- 1 ounce simple syrup (infuse with lavender)
- 3 ounces prosecco
- 1 ounce club soda
- Lavender sprigs

1. Fill a highball glass or goblet half full with ice.
2. Pour the lemon juice or limoncello and simple syrup over ice.
3. Top with prosecco and club soda.
4. Garnish with fresh lavender sprigs.

MAKE IT A MOCKTAIL

Substitute prosecco with club soda.

Love Potion No. 75
ROSE FRENCH 75

You'll have hearts for eyes as you sip on this delicious, floral potion, a rosy twist on the classic French 75! Roses have been associated with love and love goddesses like Venus and Aphrodite for millennia. This is the perfect drink to enjoy with a loved one or while romance blossoms. Although Western culture celebrates romance on Valentine's Day in the middle of winter, spring is really the season for love. They don't call it the birds and the bees for nothing, and this is truly their season as our precious pollinators!

- 1 ounce gin
- ½ ounce rose water
- ½ ounce simple syrup (infuse with rosebuds, if not using the sparkling rosé)
- 3 ounces sparkling rosé
- Dried rosebuds or petals

1. Combine the gin, rose water, and simple syrup in a shaker with ice and shake well.
2. Strain into a coupe glass.
3. Top with sparkling rosé.
4. Garnish with dried rosebuds or petals.

MAKE IT A MOCKTAIL

Substitute gin and sparkling rosé with sparkling water or club soda.

Sebastopol Mule
RHUBARB MULE

This concoction has it all: sweet, tart, fruit, and fizz! A traditional mule combines vodka, lime, and ginger beer but this springtime twist adds fresh rhubarb puree for a tart and fruity update on the classic. This mule would also make a delicious springtime adults-only popsicle if frozen (just remember not to add too much vodka, as the alcohol will not freeze completely!) Rhubarb is an oft-overlooked fruit with a short season, so don't pass it over this spring.

- 3 stalks fresh rhubarb
- ⅓ cup sugar
- 1 cup water
- 2 ounces vodka
- ½ ounce lime juice
- 3 ounces ginger beer

1. Wash and dice the fresh rhubarb and place it in a blender with the sugar and water. Blend until pureed.
2. Fill a copper mule mug or rocks glass half full with ice and the rhubarb puree.
3. Add the vodka, lime juice, and ginger beer over ice and stir.

MAKE IT A MOCKTAIL

Substitute vodka with ginger beer.

Shut Your Piehole

STRAWBERRY-RHUBARB DAIQUIRI

Daiquiris are the perfect opportunity to indulge your craving for the fruitiest cocktail option. This particular recipe combines all the fruity goodness of your favorite daiquiri with the unbeatable springtime combination of strawberries and rhubarb. There's a reason these two fruits are so frequently used together, because they really make each other shine! Paired with a little bit of sugar and white rum, this combination makes for the perfect sip.

- 4 large strawberries, plus extra for garnish
- ½ stalk rhubarb
- 2 ounces white rum
- 1 ounce simple syrup
- 1 cup ice

1. Wash and slice strawberries and rhubarb.
2. Add the chopped fruit and all remaining ingredients to a blender and blend until smooth.
3. Pour into a coupe glass.
4. Garnish with a whole strawberry, sliced to fit on the rim of the glass.

MAKE IT A MOCKTAIL

Substitute white rum with tonic water.

BASIL MOJITO

Mojitos lend themselves beautifully to herbal infusion. They're often made with mint, but this twist brings the savory, herbaceous goodness of basil to the forefront. Basil and lime is a somewhat unusual combination that just works! Basil is believed to be a sacred vessel of purification by many cultures. A few sips of this green drink might just clear your thoughts and ground you in purifying earth energy.

- 10 fresh basil leaves, divided
- 2 ounces lime juice
- 1 teaspoon sugar
- 2 ounces white rum
- 3 ounces club soda
- Lime wedge

1. Tear up half the basil leaves and muddle in a shaker with lime juice and sugar.
2. Add ice and the rum to shaker and shake well.
3. Strain into a highball glass and top with club soda.
4. Garnish with remaining basil leaves and a lime wedge.

MAKE IT A MOCKTAIL

Substitute white rum with half lime juice and half club soda.

The Tzatziki

CUCUMBER DILL GIMLET

Dill is one of my favorite spring herbs for its light and unique flavor. It pairs beautifully with lots of savory dishes, but personally, I think dill and gin are a cocktail maker's match made in heaven. Gin is the alcohol that leans heaviest on botanical flavors all on its own, so it goes wonderfully with lots of different herbs and spices. In springtime, dill is the perfect garnish to your gin cocktail of choice, but in this recipe, we take it one step further with the addition of refreshing cucumber!

- ½ cucumber
- ¼ cup fresh dill, plus extra for garnish
- 3 ounces gin
- 1 ounce lime juice
- 1 ounce simple syrup

1. Grate the cucumber on the smallest side of a cheese grater so it is pulpy, almost a puree.
2. Place fresh dill in the bottom of a shaker and muddle vigorously.
3. Add ice, the gin, lime juice, 2 tablespoons cucumber pulp, and simple syrup to the shaker and shake well.
4. Strain into a coupe glass.
5. Garnish with fresh dill.

MAKE IT A MOCKTAIL

Substitute gin with nonalcoholic gin or club soda.

Kentucky Prescription

ELDERFLOWER MINT JULEP

Elderflower liqueur is one of the best-kept secrets in the cocktail space! This unique, sophisticated ingredient can be added to all sorts of classic cocktails for a light and floral note, just right for springtime. The mint julep has a much longer tradition than most cocktails, likely invented in the eighteenth century, and the addition of elderflower liqueur makes for a charming and modern update.

- A few fresh mint leaves, plus extra for garnish
- ½ ounce simple syrup
- 2 ounces bourbon
- 1 ounce elderflower liqueur
- ANGOSTURA® bitters

1. Add the mint leaves and simple syrup to the bottom of a rocks glass and muddle gently.
2. Add the bourbon, elderflower liqueur, bitters, and a generous amount of crushed ice to the glass, then stir.
3. Garnish with fresh mint.

MAKE IT A MOCKTAIL

Add dried elderflower to simple syrup and substitute bourbon with ginger beer.

The Social Butterfly

LAVENDER GIN FIZZ

There's nothing quite as elegant or fun-loving as a gin fizz and this particular concoction introduces the playful flavor of lavender to the mix. Butterfly pea flower is a wonderful addition which colors the drink a soft and lovely hue of purple. You'll feel as light and airy as a butterfly as you toast to joy and laughter at your next garden party with this delicious treat. Gin fizzes are easier to make than they seem, so no need to save this one for a special occasion, though!

- 2 ounces butterfly pea flower gin (you can use regular gin, but the drink will not appear as purple)
- 1 ounce lemon juice
- 1 ounce simple syrup (infuse with lavender, if desired)
- 1 egg white
- Club soda, to top
- 1 sprig fresh lavender, for garnish

1. Combine the gin, lemon juice, simple syrup, and egg white in a cocktail shaker, without ice. Shake for 15 seconds.
2. Add ice to the shaker and shake until cold.
3. Strain into a coupe glass and top gently with club soda.
4. Garnish with the sprig of fresh lavender.

MAKE IT A MOCKTAIL

Add butterfly pea flower to the simple syrup for color and substitute gin with nonalcoholic gin or tonic water.

The Amelia

VODKA AVIATION

Violet isn't a flavor often found in cocktails, with the one notable exception of the gin-based Aviation, a throwback from the early twentieth century. This violet beverage brings purple flora into the twenty-first century with not just crème de violette liqueur but also fresh violets. Fresh violets have become a favorite in the edible flower crowd as an addition to fruit salads and delicate desserts, but their intense floral scent is a lovely addition to botanical cocktails as well!

- 2 ounces vodka
- 1 ounce simple syrup (infuse with fresh violets)
- 1 ounce crème de violette liqueur
- ½ ounce lemon juice
- Fresh violets, for garnish

1. Combine vodka, simple syrup, liqueur, and lemon juice in a shaker with ice. Shake well.
2. Strain into a coupe glass.
3. Garnish with fresh violets.

MAKE IT A MOCKTAIL

Substitute vodka with tonic water.

Spring Sunrise
GUAVA TEQUILA SUNRISE

Have you ever noticed how the sunrises in spring are particularly uplifting? In the weeks following the spring equinox, the days begin to grow longer than the nights, and that precious sunlight feels even more exuberant than usual. This fruity, springtime twist on a classic tequila sunrise introduces guava juice for a light pink and red drink that embodies an April sunrise.

- 2 ounces tequila
- 4 ounces guava or strawberry-guava juice
- ¼ ounce grenadine

1. Fill a highball glass with ice.
2. Add in the tequila and then the guava or strawberry-guava juice, separately, over the ice.
3. Top with the grenadine, allowing it to settle to the bottom of the glass.

MAKE IT A MOCKTAIL

Substitute tequila with club soda.

CHAPTER 5

Summer Cocktails & Mocktails

Summer is the season of lazy, hazy days in the sunshine. This is the season for taking action on our goals and making time for joy, relaxation, and abundance. If there was ever a time of year to embrace the adage "work hard, play hard," summertime is it.

Many festivals and celebrations from around the world celebrate the summer solstice, often acknowledged as the first day of summer. The solstice occurs in the northern hemisphere around June 20 (and in the southern hemisphere around December 20). This is the longest day of the year, with the most daylight hours.

Druids and pagans have gathered at Stonehenge in England for many years to witness the sunrise over the ancient stone monument. There are also monuments on practically every continent that align with the sunrise or sunset on the solstice, including Machu Picchu in Peru and Nabta Playa in Egypt. World-famous celebrations of the longest day also occur in Iceland, Sweden, and Spain. Father's Day celebrations frequently occur in the summer, honoring the men and caregivers who support us.

Later in the summer, we might celebrate Lammas, also known as

Lughnasadh, the Celtic celebration of the wheat and grain harvest on August 1. Some people also like to celebrate the Lion's Gate on August 8 (8/8), which refers to the alignment of the sun with the star, Sirius, (although the actual alignment may occur any time between late July and mid-August). In ancient Greece, the Olympic games were held in the height of summer, while the ancient Romans honored Vulcan (the god of fire) in August to prevent the burning of crops in the dry heat.

Those born under the constellations of Cancer, Leo, and Virgo also celebrate their birthdays in the summer. Those born under Cancer are sensitive, intuitive people with a strong sense of family and connection and a desire to defend those they love. Leos are bold, fierce individuals who are known for their creativity and ability to uplift and inspire. And Virgos are the facilitators of the zodiac, whether they're organizing office systems for greater efficiency or planning a group outing.

Many summertime festivities are not necessarily linked to a specific date or holiday, but are merely celebrations of the long days, warm evenings, and abundant overflowing gardens of summer. Whether we are inviting friends over for a last-minute barbecue or planning a pool or beach day picnic, summer offers myriad opportunities to celebrate, focus on the joy of connection, and break bread with loved ones.

You might find yourself in need of a vibrant summer cocktail for any of these festive celebrations and we've got you covered with twelve delicious recipes in this chapter!

> All recipes in this chapter make a
> single serving, unless otherwise noted.

Strawberry Moon Spritz

STRAWBERRY APEROL SPRITZ

Full moons throughout the year have been given names by many different cultures, including the Celts, the Chinese, and some indigenous tribes of North America. The Strawberry Moon is the Algonquin name for the full moon in June. It's always been a personal favorite of mine, conjuring up summer romance on warm, moonlit evenings. The Aperol spritz is a light and bubbly Italian summer favorite, and with the addition of fresh strawberries, it's perfect for bringing the vacation vibes all summer long.

- ¼ cup fresh strawberries, sliced, plus extra for garnish
- 1 teaspoon sugar
- 2 ounces Aperol
- 3 ounces prosecco
- 1 ounce club soda

1. Place the fresh strawberries in a glass or shaker with the sugar and muddle vigorously until the strawberries turn to pulp.
2. Fill a large wine glass or champagne flute mostly full with ice and top with the strawberry pulp.
3. Pour the Aperol over the strawberry mixture, then add the prosecco.
4. Top with the club soda.
5. Garnish with strawberry slices or a whole strawberry.

MAKE IT A MOCKTAIL

Substitute Aperol with grenadine and prosecco with club soda.

Tastes Like Pink Sangria
BERRY ROSE SANGRIA

Serves: 6

To quote *The Sound of Music*, this drink is, "Not too sour. Not too sweet. Just too, uh . . . pink." Or rather, just pink enough, with your favorite rosé wine, fresh berries, and dried rosebuds in the mix! Sangria can be made with essentially any chilled wine and sliced fruits, though the addition of a little hard alcohol, liqueur, and fizz really elevates it and is sure to bring the beach or poolside fun!

- 1 grapefruit, sliced
- 1 cup fresh strawberries, sliced
- 1 cup fresh raspberries
- 1 bottle rosé wine
- 1 cup sparkling water
- ½ cup vodka
- ½ cup orange liqueur
- ¼ cup dried rosebuds or fresh rose petals

1. Place all the fresh fruit in a large pitcher.
2. Pour the wine, sparkling water, vodka, and orange liqueur over the fruits. Stir with a wooden spoon.
3. Refrigerate for at least four hours.
4. Pour into glasses, being sure to scoop in some fruit.
5. Garnish with the dried rosebuds (or fresh rose petals!).

MAKE IT A MOCKTAIL

Substitute rosé wine and vodka with grapefruit juice and orange liqueur with orange juice.

Lavender Fields Forever

LAVENDER BLUEBERRY SMASH

This bright, cheerful recipe incorporates fresh lavender in multiple ways. You'll find lavender muddled in the drink and as a garnish, of course, but also adorning the glass itself with a delectable floral sugar rim. The touch of honey adds natural sweetness and balance. This recipe is the perfect opportunity to pay a visit to your local farmers' market to collect all the ingredients!

LAVENDER SUGAR

- ½ cup sugar
- A few fresh lavender sprigs
- Lemon wedge

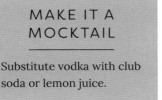

MAKE IT A MOCKTAIL

Substitute vodka with club soda or lemon juice.

COCKTAIL

- Fresh blueberries, plus extra for garnish
- A few fresh lavender sprigs, plus extra for garnish
- 1 teaspoon honey
- 2 ounces vodka
- 1 ounce lemon juice
- 2 ounces club soda

1. Place the sugar and fresh lavender buds, removed from stem, in a food processor and blend until combined.
2. Place the lavender sugar on a low, shallow plate. Wet the rim of a highball glass with a lemon wedge, then dip the rim in the sugar until it's evenly coated.
3. Place the blueberries, more fresh lavender, and honey in a shaker and muddle vigorously.
4. Add the vodka and lemon juice to shaker with ice. Shake well.
5. Strain into prepared highball glass and top with club soda.
6. Garnish with fresh lavender sprigs and blueberries.

Honey Bee Mine

JASMINE ELDERFLOWER BEE'S KNEES

This delicate, summery take on the Bee's Knees cocktail of the 1920s incorporates both jasmine and elderflower. Even if you're not a honeybee yourself, you'll be drawn to these flowers with their sweet perfume and romantic vibe. It's impossible to choose favorites, but this recipe is a particular love of mine from this book, calling on two of my favorite botanical ingredients that folklore says promote love, intimacy, and romance.

HONEY JASMINE SYRUP

- ½ cup honey
- ½ cup white sugar
- 2 tablespoons dried jasmine flowers

COCKTAIL

- 2 ounces gin
- 1 ounce lemon juice
- 1 ounce elderflower liqueur
- ½ ounce honey jasmine syrup
- Dried jasmine flowers, for garnish
- Lemon twist, for garnish

1. Combine the honey, white sugar, and dried jasmine flowers in a saucepan. Bring to a simmer. Stir, until sugar has dissolved. Let jasmine steep for 5 to 10 minutes, then strain. Allow to cool.
2. Add the gin, lemon juice, elderflower liqueur, and honey jasmine syrup to a shaker with ice. Shake well.
3. Strain into a coupe glass.
4. Garnish with dried jasmine flowers and a lemon twist.

MAKE IT A MOCKTAIL

Make honey syrup with dried jasmine flowers and dried elderflowers. Substitute gin with club soda.

Hibiscus Mojito

Hibiscus flowers are the pinnacle of tropical summery vibes. But did you know you can eat and drink them? Dried hibiscus petals are potently flavorful and add vibrant color to beverages of all kinds. In this recipe, we're making a hibiscus infusion, then adding it to all the ingredients for a classic mojito. Hibiscus pairs beautifully with the island flavors of white rum and lime—and always makes for a visually stunning presentation.

- Dried hibiscus petals
- 3 ounces white rum
- 2 ounces lime juice
- 1 teaspoon sugar
- 2 ounces club soda
- Lime wedge, for garnish

1. Place hibiscus petals in a tea bag or tea infuser and infuse in 1 cup hot water for 2 to 4 minutes. Add ice and chill hibiscus infusion.
2. Pour the rum, lime juice, sugar, and 2 ounces chilled hibiscus infusion into a shaker with ice and shake well.
3. Strain into a highball glass and top with club soda.
4. Garnish with a lime wedge.

MAKE IT A MOCKTAIL

Substitute white rum with half hibiscus infusion and half lime juice.

Savannah Nights

PEACH SPRITZ

I spent a little time in Savannah, Georgia, a few years ago in the height of July. No, not the traditionally ideal time of year to visit the American South! Despite my usual distaste for the heat, though, I was surprised to find the hot, humid nights positively romantic. I could easily imagine sipping on this summery spritz made with fresh thyme and peaches while wandering through Forsyth Park at twilight, listening to the splash of the fountain, live jazz, and hooting of an owl in the oak and magnolia trees overhead.

- A few fresh sprigs thyme, plus extra for garnish
- 2 ounces peach schnapps
- 3 ounces prosecco
- 1 ounce club soda
- Fresh peach slice

1. Place sprigs of fresh thyme at the bottom of a large wine glass or champagne flute.
2. Fill the glass mostly full with ice and pour the peach schnapps over the ice.
3. Pour the prosecco over the ice and top with club soda.
4. Garnish with a fresh peach slice and fresh thyme.

MAKE IT A MOCKTAIL

Substitute prosecco with club soda and peach schnapps with simple syrup (infuse with fresh peaches, if desired).

Kick It Up a Notch
SPICY PINEAPPLE MARGARITA

This fruity margarita kicks it up a notch with not only vibrant tropical fruit but also tajin and chili powder to boot! The margarita itself starts with pureed pineapple chunks, so creamy and thick all on their own that it's practically homemade Dole Whip®. (In fact, I'd happily swap in this drink for the real thing at my next visit to the Enchanted Tiki Room at Disneyland!) Pineapple then meets its match with tequila, lime, and a spicy sea salt rim. You could also easily make this into a blended margarita by blending all the ingredients with ice.

SALT RIM
- Medium coarse sea salt
- 1 teaspoon tajin and/or chili powder
- Lime wedge

COCKTAIL
- 1 cup fresh pineapple chunks
- 2 ounces tequila
- 1 ounce orange liqueur
- 1 ounce lime juice
- Pineapple slice, for garnish (cut out star shape with a miniature cookie cutter, if desired)

1. Place the sea salt and tajin and/or chili powder on a low, shallow plate. Wet the rim of a rocks glass with a lime wedge, then dip the rim in the salt until it's evenly coated.
2. Place the pineapple chunks in a blender and blend until pureed.
3. Fill a shaker with ice and combine tequila, orange liqueur, and lime juice. Shake well.

(continued ...)

4. Fill prepared glass with ice and pineapple puree, then strain the contents of the shaker into it. Stir to combine.

5. Garnish with a slice of pineapple.

MAKE IT A MOCKTAIL

Substitute tequila and orange liqueur with orange juice.

Marjoram Paloma

The paloma is one of my favorite summer cocktails, sort of like a grapefruit twist on a margarita. It lends itself wonderfully to lots of different flavor combinations in all different seasons. For summer, we're introducing an herbal note to this citrusy delight. You might expect to find marjoram in your chili or pasta sauce rather than in your paloma glass, but this fragrant herb brings out a note of depth and complexity even in a cocktail.

SALT RIM
- Medium coarse sea salt
- Lime wedge

COCKTAIL
- A few fresh marjoram sprigs, plus extra for garnish
- 1 ounce lime juice, divided
- 2 ounces grapefruit juice
- 2 ounces tequila
- Agave nectar, to taste

1. Place the sea salt on a low, shallow plate. Wet the rim of a rocks glass with a lime wedge, then dip the rim in the salt until it's evenly coated.
2. Place the fresh marjoram in a shaker with ½ ounce lime juice and muddle vigorously to release the scent and flavor of the herbs. Strain.
3. Fill the prepared glass half full with ice.
4. Pour in the grapefruit juice, tequila, remaining lime juice, and agave nectar. Stir.
5. Garnish with fresh marjoram sprigs.

MAKE IT A MOCKTAIL

Substitute tequila with club soda.

Summer Storm Clouds

BLACKBERRY THYME DARK 'N STORMY

I sipped on my first Dark 'n Stormy at a little Welsh pub in what's known as the "town of books," a tiny hamlet called Hay-on-Wye that's replete with more than twenty bookstores of varying sizes and genres. It was the perfect match for the Welsh weather and the sheer romance of spending three straight days browsing bookshelves and ducking under seventeenth-century doorways. This fruity, herbal twist on the classic Dark 'n Stormy achieves the same layered appearance with not only dark rum but fresh blackberries as well.

- A few fresh thyme leaves, plus extra for garnish
- ½ ounce lime juice
- A few fresh blackberries, plus extra for garnish
- 2 ounces dark rum
- 3 ounces ginger beer

1. Muddle the thyme leaves with the lime juice in a shaker, smashing together.
2. Add in the blackberries and muddle for another 1 to 2 minutes.
3. Add in the rum and shake well.
4. Fill a highball glass ²/₃ full with ice, then pour in the ginger beer.
5. Strain shaker over ice and ginger beer.
6. Garnish with a fresh blackberry and thyme sprig.

MAKE IT A MOCKTAIL

Substitute dark rum with iced black tea.

Sunset Campfire
CALENDULA MEZCAL MULE

Calendula is a bright and sunny orange flower that's related to marigold. Calendula is a favorite flower among herbalists for everything from tea to skincare products, not only because it is deeply healing and anti-inflammatory, but also because of its lovely color and appearance. This smoky twist on the classic mule marries the summery flavors of tequila, ginger, and lime with fresh calendula, introducing a tangy note.

- 2 ounces mezcal
- ½ ounce lime juice
- ½ ounce simple syrup (infuse with calendula petals)
- 3 ounces ginger beer
- Fresh calendula flowers, for garnish

1. Fill a copper mule mug or a rocks glass half full with ice.
2. Add the mezcal, lime juice, and simple syrup over ice. Stir.
3. Top with ginger beer.
4. Garnish with fresh calendula flowers.

MAKE IT A MOCKTAIL

Substitute mezcal with iced chai or ginger beer.

Sage Wisdom

Mead is honey wine, often made sparkling. It's delicious when sipped chilled on its own, but it also makes a delightful addition to cocktails. This recipe combines mead with bourbon, so it's actually quite strong! The honeyed wine mellows the bourbon, while the herbaceous flavor of sage leaves brings in an earthy quality. This cocktail reminds me of cool evenings in late summer when the sun has just dipped below the horizon.

- 1 tablespoon simple syrup (infuse with sage)
- Dash ANGOSTURA® bitters
- 2 ounces bourbon
- 2 ounces mead
- Fresh sage leaves, for garnish

1. Add the simple syrup and bitters to a shaker and stir to combine.
2. Fill shaker with ice and the bourbon. Stir.
3. Place a large ice cube in a rocks glass and strain shaker over it.
4. Top with the mead.
5. Garnish with the fresh sage leaves.

MAKE IT A MOCKTAIL

Substitute bourbon with iced black tea and mead with sparkling cider.

Iced Dandelion Root Rum and "Coke"

Serves: 12

This recipe takes the classic and very simple rum and coke cocktail to epically botanical heights. First, we start with a dandelion root sun tea—an herbal tisane steeped in cold water and brewed by the heat of the summer sun. Dandelion root tea is often enjoyed as a coffee substitute because it is so darkly colored and flavored. With the addition of fizzy club soda, it also makes a lovely substitute for your favorite carbonated beverage, perfect for use in a refreshing rum and botanical "coke."

- 3 tablespoons roasted dandelion root (dried herb)
- 8 cups cold water
- 2 cups dark rum
- 2 cups club soda

1. Fill three empty tea bags or a large tea infuser with the dandelion root.
2. Add the cold water to a pitcher or a large mason jar with a lid. Submerge the tea bags or infuser in the water and close the lid.
3. Place outside in a warm, sunny spot where the pitcher will be undisturbed for at least a few hours. Allow the tea to slowly steep until it is to your taste.
4. Bring the pitcher or jar inside, discard the tea bags or infuser, and place in the refrigerator to chill for at least an hour.
5. In a fresh pitcher, combine the chilled dandelion root tea and rum. Stir to combine.
6. Top with club soda.

MAKE IT A MOCKTAIL

Substitute dark rum with ginger beer or club soda.

CHAPTER 6

Autumn Cocktails & Mocktails

Autumn is the season of winding down, turning within, and celebrating the hard work we've put in throughout the year. This is the season of harvest and gratitude. There is a coziness and a warmth to fall that asks us to focus on what feels nourishing, comforting, and deep.

There are festivals and celebrations from around the world that celebrate fall as a time of harvest, intuition, and magic. Many of them are linked to the autumn equinox in some way. The equinox occurs each year in the northern hemisphere around September 20 (and in the southern hemisphere around March 20). This is one of two days a year when day and night are equal and balanced—from this point forward until the solstice, the nights grow longer than the days.

The Moon Festival in China occurs on the full moon closest to the autumn equinox and celebrates the harvest. The ancient Celts celebrated the equinox as a day of harvest and gratitude, which has been revived by neo-pagans, sometimes under the name Mabon (which is actually the name of a Welsh god). The Jewish holiday of Sukkot also occurs in the weeks surrounding the equinox in late September or October and celebrates the harvest.

Later in the fall, many of us celebrate Halloween on October 31, a day of sweets, merriment, and costumes. But did you know this fun holiday has its roots in the ancient Celtic festival of Samhain? One of the most sacred holidays in Celtic culture, Samhain is believed to be the night when the veil becomes thin between our human world and the realm of the dead, allowing spirits and ancestors to pass into our world to provide guidance—and create mischief.

Samhain is not the only fall festival that honors the dead. Día de los Muertos is celebrated on November 1 in Mexico and other Latin American countries and involves honoring the dead with altars called ofrendas, decorated with marigolds, photos, mementos of those of who have passed on, and elaborate painted skulls. Ohigan is the Japanese celebration of remembering and honoring ancestors, which occurs on both equinoxes in March and September. In Canada and the United States, we circle back to the theme of gratitude later in the fall with our Thanksgiving celebrations in October and November.

Those born under the constellations of Libra, Scorpio, and Sagittarius also celebrate their birthdays in the fall. Those born under Libra are artistic, fair-minded folks with an eye for beauty and a gift for mediation. Scorpios are deep, mysterious people who value transformation and are unafraid of the taboos in life. And Sagittarians are the adventurers of the zodiac, always off exploring, whether it be a new culture, a new degree, a new relationship, or a new spiritual path.

You might find yourself in need of a cozy autumn cocktail for any of these festive celebrations and we've got you covered with thirteen delicious recipes in this chapter!

All recipes in this chapter make a single serving, unless otherwise noted.

Perfect Fall Pair

BRANDIED PEAR SMASH

This is one of few recipes in this book that requires a couple days of preparation ahead of time, but believe me, it's worth it! Pears and brandy go together beautifully this time of year, when the leaves are changing, the weather has cooled, and you're longing for a cozy night in. Pear liqueur really brings that fall fruit flavor forward and is delicious in all kinds of fall drinks and desserts as well!

- 2 fresh pears, peeled and sliced
- 1 cup brandy
- 2 teaspoons ground cinnamon
- ¼ cup brown sugar
- 1 ounce pear liqueur
- ½ ounce lemon juice
- 2 ounces club soda
- Cinnamon stick, for garnish

1. Place peeled pear slices in a medium-sized mason jar. Cover with brandy, ground cinnamon, and brown sugar.
2. Refrigerate for at least 2 to 3 days, but up to a week, to infuse.
3. Remove brandied pears from the refrigerator, place in a bowl, and mash the pears with the back of a wooden spoon.
4. Add 2 ounces brandied pear mash to a shaker with the liqueur, lemon juice, and ice. Shake well.
5. Strain into a rocks glass and top with club soda.
6. Garnish with a cinnamon stick.

MAKE IT A MOCKTAIL

Cook pears down on the stove with the cinnamon and brown sugar before mashing. Substitute pear liqueur with simple syrup (infuse with pears, if desired).

The Persnickety

PERSIMMON BELLINI

Persimmons are one of those unique fruits that no one ever seems to know what to do with! Although they can be delicious baked into breads and tarts, or even sliced on top of a fall salad, I think we've officially discovered the best new use of these bright orange enigmas: blended into a Bellini! The classic Bellini is made with peaches, much more of a summery vibe, but persimmons bring this treat right into the crisp, cool days of fall.

- Fresh Fuyu persimmon
- 1 tablespoon orange juice
- 1 ounce cognac or brandy
- 6 ounces sparkling wine

1. Peel and chop persimmon into chunks and blend into a puree.
2. Add persimmon puree to the bottom of a champagne flute.
3. Top with orange juice and cognac or brandy, then sparkling wine.

MAKE IT A MOCKTAIL

Substitute sparkling wine with club soda and cognac or brandy with apple juice.

Figgy Gin and Jam

Did you know you can combine your favorite jam with gin and lemon juice for a simple, fun, and totally customizable cocktail? This recipe couldn't be easier. You could certainly use jam of any variety here, but fig jam and fresh figs really elevate this ridiculously simple drink. Figs are a wonderful pairing with the herbal note of gin, which is made with juniper berries and botanicals of all kinds.

- 2 ounces gin
- ½ ounce lemon juice
- 2 tablespoons fig jam
- Fresh fig slice, for garnish

1. Add the gin, lemon juice, jam, and ice to a shaker. Stir first to break up the jam, then shake vigorously until all ingredients are combined.
2. Strain into a coupe glass.
3. Garnish with a fresh fig slice.

MAKE IT A MOCKTAIL

Substitute gin with tonic water.

Ophelia's Legacy
ROSEMARY OLD FASHIONED

It's not called an old fashioned for nothing—this is the original cocktail, just bourbon, sugar, and bitters—but with a botanical twist, of course! Fresh rosemary brings bring out the complexity of the bourbon here. Folklore, and even Shakespeare, tell us that rosemary is for honoring legacy and remembering those who came before. This rosemary old fashioned does just that, honoring the original cocktail while introducing it to the botanical approach of the modern era.

- 1 ounce simple syrup (infuse with fresh rosemary)
- 3 dashes ANGOSTURA® or rosemary bitters
- 2 ounces bourbon
- 1 sprig fresh rosemary, for garnish
- Orange twist, for garnish

1. Add the simple syrup and bitters to a shaker and stir to combine.
2. Fill shaker with ice and add bourbon. Stir.
3. Place a large ice cube in a rocks glass and strain shaker over it.
4. Garnish with a sprig of rosemary and an orange twist.

MAKE IT A MOCKTAIL

Substitute bourbon with iced black tea.

Blood Moon

One of the most evocative full moon names of the year is October's Blood Moon, although this spooky title is also given to lunar eclipses, when the earth's shadow falls across the face of the full moon, turning it a dusky red. This cocktail in honor of the Blood Moon is perfect for your Halloween girls' night, bringing together a bevy of unique and vibrantly colored ingredients. Pomegranate and blood orange both make an appearance, as do rose hips, often collected by herbalists after the first frost.

- 1 blood orange, sliced, plus extra for garnish
- 1 ounce simple syrup (infuse with rose hips, if desired) or rose hip liqueur
- 2 ounces pomegranate juice
- 2 ounces dark rum
- Dried rose petals, for garnish

1. Remove the rind from two slices of the blood orange and place in a shaker with the simple syrup or liqueur. Muddle vigorously.
2. Add the pomegranate juice and rum and shake well.
3. Strain into a coupe glass.
4. Garnish with a blood orange wedge and dried rose petals.

MAKE IT A MOCKTAIL

Substitute rum with iced black tea.

Persephone's Brew
SPICED POMEGRANATE WHISKEY PUNCH

Serves: 4

Pomegranates ripen right around Halloween. The ancient Greeks associated pomegranates with Persephone, the goddess of vegetation, because pomegranate seeds tied her to fate as queen alongside Hades in the Underworld. This punch would be just right for welcoming Persephone back to the Underworld . . . or for a warm treat after trick-or-treating in the cold!

- 1 whole pomegranate
- 4 cups cold water
- 1 fresh rosemary sprig
- 5 black peppercorns
- 8 whole cloves
- 2 cardamom pods
- 1 cinnamon stick
- 1 cup whiskey

1. Rinse the pomegranate well and cut into quarters. Place in a saucepan and cover with cold water.
2. Bring to a boil. Reduce heat, add the sprig of fresh rosemary, and simmer for 3 to 7 minutes, depending on taste.
3. Combine all the spices in a tea infuser or cheesecloth sack and add to the saucepan. Discard the pomegranate quarters and rosemary sprig and simmer for another 10 to 15 minutes, until the water is dark and flavorful.
4. Add whiskey and stir. Reduce heat and serve warm.

MAKE IT A MOCKTAIL

Substitute whiskey with ½ cup water.

Witch's Cauldron

TRIPLE SPICED PUMPKIN PUNCH

Serves: 8

This punch is sure to be a hit at your next fall gathering, whether it's at the autumn equinox, Halloween, Thanksgiving, or anytime in between! It takes a bit of prep work to make your own pumpkin butter and chai from scratch, but the potency of the fresh flavors is worth the effort. It brings together all the warm and cozy scents of fall with spiced rum and brandy for a smooth, delicious sip.

PUMPKIN BUTTER

- ½ cup pumpkin puree
- 1 cup dark brown sugar
- 1 cup water
- 2 teaspoons ground cinnamon
- 1 teaspoon ground clove
- 1 teaspoon ground cardamom
- Pinch salt

CHAI SPICES

- 1 cinnamon stick
- 3–5 whole cloves
- 2–3 whole cardamom pods, gently crushed
- 1 whole star anise

COCKTAIL

- 1 cup pumpkin butter
- 2 cups chilled chai
- 1 cup spiced rum
- 1 cup brandy
- 1 cup chilled ginger beer
- Cinnamon sticks and cloves, for garnish

1. Combine all pumpkin butter ingredients in a small saucepan. Bring to a simmer over low heat and cook for 5 minutes. Remove from heat and allow to cool.

(continued . . .)

2. Place all chai spices in a tea bag or tea infuser and infuse in 2 cups hot water for 5 to 10 minutes. Chill in the refrigerator.
3. In a punch bowl or pitcher, whisk together the pumpkin butter, chilled chai, rum, and brandy until the pumpkin has dissolved.
4. Pour the ginger beer into the bowl or pitcher and stir gently.
5. Garnish with cinnamon sticks and cloves.

MAKE IT A MOCKTAIL

Substitute rum and brandy with half ginger beer and half chai.

Listen to Your Elder (Trees)

ELDERBERRY FRENCH 75

It seems that every part of the elder tree is potent and delicious, from the delicate flowers to the immune-boosting berries. Although elderberries are poisonous when eaten raw, after being dried or cooked, they become staples of every herbalist's cabinet in the fall and winter months. They're often made into a healthy, delicious syrup, which we're combining here with three kinds of alcohol, each with its own unique flavor and character.

- 1 ounce gin
- ½ ounce elderflower liqueur
- ½ ounce elderberry syrup
- 3 ounces sparkling wine

1. Combine the gin, elderflower liqueur, and syrup in a shaker with ice and shake well.
2. Strain into a champagne flute.
3. Top with sparkling wine.

MAKE IT A MOCKTAIL

Substitute gin and sparkling wine with sparkling water or club soda. Substitute elderflower liqueur with iced tea made with elderflowers.

Autumn Spiced Cider Sangria

Serves: 6

We often think of sangria, the chilled fruit and wine favorite of Spain, in summer, but with the addition of spices and apple cider, it's perfect for your fall table as well. This delicious blend honors the fall harvest with some of your favorite autumn seasonal fruits, such as apple and pear, along with a medley of classic fall spices. The full-bodied flavor of the red wine mingles with the fruit and spiced warmth of the cider for a delicious harvest treat.

- 1 orange, sliced
- 2 apples, sliced
- 1 pear, chopped
- 3–5 cinnamon sticks, plus extra for garnish
- 1 tablespoon whole cloves
- 1–2 whole star anises
- 1 bottle red wine

- ½ cup brandy
- 1 cup apple cider
- ¼ cup orange juice

CINNAMON-SUGAR RIM

- 2 tablespoons white sugar
- 1 tablespoon ground cinnamon

1. Place the prepared fruit in a large pitcher.
2. Add the whole spices.
3. Pour the wine, brandy, cider, and orange juice over the fruits and spices. Stir with a wooden spoon.
4. Refrigerate for at least four hours.
5. Place the cinnamon-sugar rim ingredients on a low, shallow plate. Wet the rim of a stemless wine glass, then dip in the sugar so that the rim is evenly coated.
6. Pour into prepared glasses and garnish with a cinnamon stick.

MAKE IT A MOCKTAIL

Substitute red wine with grape juice or nonalcoholic wine. Substitute brandy with orange juice.

Apple Orchard
TRIPLE APPLE WHISKEY SIPPER

If you've ever wanted to wander through an apple orchard on a crisp fall day with a picnic basket and a plaid shawl drawn around your shoulders, this cocktail is the cottagecore beverage of your apple-picking daydreams! Combining fresh apple slices, apple juice, and hard apple cider, (fermented apple juice), with whiskey and spices, this drink is just what October ordered.

- 3 ounces apple juice
- 1 cinnamon stick
- 3–5 whole cloves
- 2 ounces whiskey
- 2 ounces hard apple cider
- Fresh apple slice, for garnish

1. Place the apple juice in a shaker with the cinnamon stick and cloves and allow the flavors to mingle for at least 5 to 10 minutes. Alternatively, bring these ingredients to a simmer on the stove for 5 to 10 minutes, strain, and allow to cool before adding to shaker.
2. Add the whiskey to shaker with ice and shake well.
3. Strain into a rocks glass.
4. Top with hard apple cider.
5. Garnish with a fresh apple slice.

MAKE IT A MOCKTAIL

Substitute whiskey with apple juice and hard cider with sparkling nonalcoholic cider.

Smoke and Magic Mirrors
SMOKY APPLE SAGE MARGARITA

I'm a big fan of smoky drinks and am particularly at home with a glass of Scotch in hand. When I had mezcal for the first time, a smoky tequila, I was sold! It pairs beautifully with spiced and herbal flavors, perfect for an autumn margarita on the rocks. In fact, now I make a pitcher of this delicious blend for all my fall gatherings and girls' nights, especially our annual pumpkin carving and *Practical Magic* viewing parties.

SPICED SALT
- 1 tablespoon medium coarse sea salt
- 1 tablespoon brown sugar
- 1 teaspoon ground cinnamon
- Lime wedge

COCKTAIL
- A few fresh sage leaves, plus extra for garnish
- 2 ounces mezcal
- ½ ounce orange liqueur
- 4 ounces apple cider
- ½ ounce lime juice
- Lime wedges
- Apple slice, for garnish
- Cinnamon stick, for garnish

1. Place the sea salt, brown sugar, and cinnamon on a low, shallow plate. Wet the rim of a rocks glass with a lime wedge, then dip the rim in the salt, sugar, and cinnamon until the rim is evenly coated.
2. Place the fresh sage leaves in a shaker and muddle to release the juices and fragrance.

(continued . . .)

3. Pour the mezcal, orange liqueur, apple cider, and lime juice into the shaker. Add ice and shake well.
4. Strain into the prepared glass.
5. Garnish with an apple slice, a cinnamon stick, and fresh sage leaves.

MAKE IT A MOCKTAIL

Substitute mezcal and orange liqueur with apple cider. To achieve a smoky flavor, smoke a few sage leaves in the overturned glass before wetting the rim of the glass.

Fennel Negroni

The Negroni is a classic Italian cocktail, an aperitif meant to be sipped before the main evening meal. When I was a kid, growing up with my Italian-American family on my mom's side, we would get fresh fennel (also called anise) from the grocery store, slice the bulb, and dip the slices in salt. (Try it, it's delicious!) This botanical twist on the Negroni brings in the entire vegetable, from the bulb to the seeds to the fronds—perhaps a grown-up version of my childhood snack.

- ½ cup finely chopped fennel bulb
- 2 teaspoons fennel seeds
- 1 ounce sweet vermouth
- 1 ounce gin
- 1 ounce Campari
- Fennel fronds, for garnish

1. Add the chopped fennel bulb and fennel seeds to a shaker with sweet vermouth and smash vigorously.
2. Add gin and Campari to the shaker with ice and stir.
3. Strain into a rocks glass with a large ice cube.
4. Garnish with fresh fennel fronds.

MAKE IT A MOCKTAIL

Substitute sweet vermouth with store-bought orange blossom water and muddle the fennel with the orange blossom water instead. Substitute gin and Campari with club soda.

Ancestral Tribute

Autumn is the season of ancestors and honoring the dead in many different cultures. Raising a glass to your ancestors or even pouring one out or setting an empty seat at the table as an offering are all excellent ways to celebrate this season.

An ancestral tribute could be made with a beverage that a deceased loved one particularly enjoyed or with a beverage that originates in your ancestral cultures. My ancestors were primarily from Scotland and northern Italy so a finger of Scotch or a glass of red wine are my ancestral drinks of choice.

CHAPTER 7

Winter Cocktails & Mocktails

Winter is the season of rest, rejuvenation, and darkness. This is the time of year when we get grounded in our homes and sources of comfort, turning to where there is light and warmth, a respite from the cold and dark outside.

So many festivals and celebrations from around the world celebrate the midpoint of winter as a time of promise that the sun will return. Many of these are linked to the winter solstice in some way. The solstice occurs each year in the northern hemisphere around December 20 (and in the southern hemisphere around June 20). This is the longest night of the year, with the least number of daylight hours.

Most of the winter solstice festivals are centered around the concept of bringing light to the darkness, literally and figuratively. This is because after the solstice, the days will slowly begin to get longer and brighter once more. Yule is the ancient Nordic, Germanic, and Celtic festival that we associate with this time of year, which involves decorating evergreen trees and boughs, lighting bonfires, and exchanging gifts. Saturnalia was the ancient Roman festival of the solstice, honoring the god of time and agriculture.

All around the world we find examples of winter holidays that incorporate candles, bonfires, and now electricity to light up the darkest nights of the year. Many also incorporate mythology about the birth or rebirth of the sun or of particular gods and goddesses, as well as ways of lighting up our hearts with gifts and song.

In modern times, we celebrate the New Year in winter, ringing in the beginning of a fresh start in the cold depths of January, not long after the solstice. Once again, this festival is about bringing light and good cheer to the darkness and looking ahead to the return of longer days.

Later in the winter, we might find ourselves celebrating Imbolc, the Celtic festival that celebrates the first signs that spring will return once more. There is also, of course, Valentine's Day in February which celebrates love of all kinds, especially romantic love, and may have its roots in the ancient Roman fertility festival of Lupercalia.

Those born under the constellations of Capricorn, Aquarius, and Pisces also celebrate their birthdays in the winter. Those born under Capricorn are grounded, practical individuals with a head for legacy and tradition. Aquarians are idea people with a quirky outlook on life and deeply ingrained sense of justice. And Pisceans are the intuitive mermaids of the zodiac, tapping into deep wells of compassion and empathy for those around them.

You might find yourself in need of a comforting winter cocktail for any of these festive celebrations and we've got you covered with twelve delicious recipes in this chapter!

All recipes in this chapter make a single serving, unless otherwise noted.

Blood Orange Sidecar

My signature cocktail for many years was a sidecar. It's classy, something a little different but easy to make, and satisfies my sweet tooth. This wintry twist features blood orange juice instead of lemon juice, introducing a bolder and more vibrant flavor and color. It's perfectly delicious with brandy but I highly recommend trying it with cognac for an elevated experience. Garnish the rim with not just sugar but a bit of orange zest and you have a truly striking—and delicious—winter option!

SUGAR RIM

- 1 tablespoon sugar
- Orange zest

COCKTAIL

- 2 ounces cognac or brandy
- 1 ounce orange liqueur
- 1 ounce blood orange juice

1. Place the sugar rim ingredients on a low, shallow plate. Wet the rim of a coupe glass, then dip the rim in the sugar until it's evenly coated.
2. Add the cognac or brandy, orange liqueur, and blood orange juice to a shaker with ice and shake well.
3. Strain into prepared coupe glass.

MAKE IT A MOCKTAIL

Substitute brandy with chilled black tea.

Trimming the Tree
POMEGRANATE MARTINI

This pomegranate martini is the signature cocktail at one of my best friend's mom's Christmas tree trimming parties every year *(thanks to Christine for the recipe!)*. It's festive for the holiday season in both color and garnish, as it's topped with either robust fresh cranberries or glittering pomegranate seeds . . . or both! Serve these delicious martinis at your next winter gathering—they'll bring a little color and vibrancy to every party from Christmas to Valentine's Day.

- 2 ounces vodka
- 1 ounce Grand Marnier
- 2 ounces pomegranate juice
- Splash lime juice
- Fresh cranberries or pomegranate seeds

1. Place the vodka, Grand Marnier, pomegranate juice, and lime juice in a shaker with ice. Shake well.
2. Strain into a martini glass.
3. Garnish with fresh cranberries or pomegranate seeds.

MAKE IT A MOCKTAIL

Substitute vodka with club soda and Grand Marnier with orange juice concentrate or a few drops of orange extract.

Brandy Orange Blossom

ORANGE POMANDER

This drink is named for the delightful holiday decoration that originated in the Middle Ages: oranges stuck with whole cloves and other spices to perfume the air. In cocktail form, the orange pomander integrates citrus flavors in multiple ways, including piquant orange blossom water. Meanwhile, the combination of brandy and rum enlivens the senses. Perhaps sip this concoction while stringing together garlands of orange slices and popcorn for the tree and listening to your favorite holiday tunes!

- 2 ounces brandy
- ½ ounce spiced rum
- ½ ounce orange liqueur
- ½ ounce store-bought orange blossom water
- ½ ounce simple syrup
- 1 ounce club soda
- Dehydrated orange slice

1. Combine the brandy, rum, orange liqueur, orange blossom water, and simple syrup in a shaker. Shake well.
2. Strain into a coupe glass.
3. Top with club soda.
4. Garnish with a dehydrated orange slice.

MAKE IT A MOCKTAIL

Substitute brandy and rum with chilled black tea. Leave out orange liqueur and infuse simple syrup with orange zest instead, if desired.

Cranberry Bog

CRANBERRY LIME MULE

This festive cocktail is perfect for bringing a little cheer to any winter evening! A classic Moscow Mule may seem more inclined toward a hot summer night, but cranberry juice invites this drink to take a seat at your holiday table. In fact, the bright, spirited flavors of lime, ginger, and cranberry are sure to make your next festivity sparkle.

- 2 ounces vodka
- ½ ounce lime juice
- 3 ounces ginger beer
- 2 ounces cranberry juice
- Fresh cranberries, for garnish
- Lime wedge, for garnish

1. Fill a copper mule mug or rocks glass half full with ice.
2. Pour the vodka, lime juice, ginger beer, and cranberry juice over ice.
3. Garnish with fresh cranberries and a lime wedge.

MAKE IT A MOCKTAIL

Substitute vodka with half ginger beer and half cranberry juice.

Wassailing Time

MULLED WINE

Serves: 6

You really cannot get more classic at the holidays (or all winter long) than with a steaming cup of mulled wine. We tend to associate mulled wine with the Victorian era, or maybe even the Middle Ages, but in fact, it originated even further back to ancient Rome! Wine heated with warming spices certainly warms the soul, and the addition of apple cider, brandy, and orange liqueur in this particular recipe really highlights the complexity of flavors present here.

- 1 bottle red wine
- 1 cup apple cider
- ¼ cup brandy
- ¼ cup orange liqueur
- 3 cinnamon sticks
- 8–10 whole cloves
- 1 blood orange, sliced
- 1 whole star anise
- Lime wedges, for garnish

1. Pour the wine, cider, brandy, and orange liqueur into a large pot on the stove over medium-low heat.
2. Add in the spices and prepared blood orange.
3. Simmer until hot and flavors are mingled.
4. Ladle into mugs or glasses and serve warm.
5. Garnish each glass with a lime wedge.

MAKE IT A MOCKTAIL

Substitute red wine, brandy, and orange liqueur with grape juice and/or nonalcoholic wine.

Intercontinental Delight

SUMAC PALOMA

Sumac, pomegranate, rose water . . . sounds like the menu at your favorite Middle Eastern restaurant, right? We're mixing these delicious ingredients with tequila, lime, and grapefruit for an intercontinental beverage that's sure to brighten the grayest winter day. We're infusing the simple syrup with sumac, a sour red spice, and adding just a hint of rose water to complement the lime juice. There is a lot going on in this drink, but every ingredient shines.

SPICED SALT

- Medium coarse pink Himalayan sea salt
- Ground sumac
- Lime wedge

COCKTAIL

- 2 ounces grapefruit juice
- 2 ounces tequila
- ½ ounce lime juice
- ½ ounce rose water
- 1 ounce simple syrup (infuse with sumac)
- Fresh pomegranate seeds, for garnish

1. Place the sea salt and ground sumac on a low, shallow plate. Wet the rim of a rocks glass with a lime wedge, then dip the rim in the salt and sumac until it's evenly coated.
2. Fill the prepared glass half full with ice.
3. Pour in the grapefruit juice, tequila, lime juice, rose water, and simple syrup. Stir.
4. Garnish with pomegranate seeds.

MAKE IT A MOCKTAIL

Substitute tequila with club soda.

Hibiscus Chai Hot Toddy

I'll be honest, the hot toddy has never been my go-to winter beverage. It always reminds me of drinking hot lemon water when I had a cold as a kid. However, you just might catch me brewing up a cup of this hibiscus toddy this winter—or a few! Hibiscus blends surprisingly well with traditional chai spices, especially cinnamon. When paired with the classic whiskey, lemon, and honey of a hot toddy, you have a winter beverage worth writing home about.

HIBISCUS CHAI

- 1 teaspoon dried hibiscus petals
- 1 cinnamon stick
- 3–5 whole cloves
- 2–3 whole cardamom pods, gently crushed
- 1 whole star anise

COCKTAIL

- ¾ cup brewed hibiscus chai
- 2 ounces whiskey
- 1 ounce lemon juice
- 2 tablespoons honey
- Cinnamon stick, for garnish

1. Place all hibiscus chai ingredients in a tea bag or tea infuser and infuse in hot water for 2 to 4 minutes.
2. Add the brewed hibiscus chai, whiskey, lemon juice, and honey to a mug and stir.
3. Garnish with a cinnamon stick.

MAKE IT A MOCKTAIL

Stir lemon juice and honey directly into brewed hibiscus chai.

Snowed In

CARDAMOM OAT MILK WHITE RUSSIAN

Cardamom is one of my favorite, often overlooked spices. It's softer and more subtle than most other spices typically found in fall and winter blends, and it pairs nicely with cozy and creamy flavors. The seeds inside of the green pods are where the flavor lies, so it's important to gently crush the pods until they pop open. For this recipe, we're steeping the gentle cardamom flavor into sweet and nourishing oat milk, a pairing made for warm winter nights by the fire.

- 5–10 cardamom pods
- 2 cups oat milk
- 2 ounces vodka
- 1 ounce Kahlúa
- Ground cardamom, for garnish
- Ground nutmeg, for garnish

1. Gently crush cardamom pods in a mortar and pestle so that the pods pop open.
2. In a small saucepan, combine the cardamom pods and oat milk over medium heat.
3. Bring to a gentle simmer and remove saucepan from heat. Allow to steep 10 to 20 minutes, to taste.
4. Strain oat milk and chill in the refrigerator.
5. Fill a rocks glass half full with ice.
6. Add the vodka and Kahlúa.
7. Top with a splash of the cardamom-infused oat milk.
8. Garnish with the ground cardamom and nutmeg.

MAKE IT A MOCKTAIL

Substitute vodka and Kahlúa with chilled brewed coffee.

Homemade Winter Gin

Makes: 1 (375-milliliter) bottle

Several years ago, my roommate and I received a gin-making kit for Christmas. The kit called for a bottle of vodka and provided a tin of juniper berries and spices to infuse it with. We started making bottles of our own gin, first with the provided botanicals and then with our own inspired mixes. It was so much fun and so delicious that we started making extras to give as gifts! Making your own gin in this way is beyond simple and a fun way to really get hands-on with the ways that alcohol and botanicals can play together.

- 2 tablespoons juniper berries
- 1 (375-milliliter) bottle high-quality vodka
- 2 teaspoons whole coriander
- 2 teaspoons angelica root
- 1 cinnamon stick
- Peel of 1 lemon
- Peel of 1 orange
- 1 sprig fresh edible evergreen such as pine, fir, or spruce (if not available, substitute rosemary)

1. Place the juniper berries in a large pitcher or jar with a lid and cover with the vodka. Seal lid and place in a cool, dark spot to infuse for approximately 12 hours.
2. Add the rest of the ingredients, submerging the evergreen sprig. Seal the lid and infuse for thirty-six hours.
3. Strain into the original vodka bottle or another jar.
4. Use for any gin cocktail or sip on its own!

MAKE IT A MOCKTAIL

Follow this same process but substitute vodka with club soda. This is an excellent nonalcoholic substitute for all your favorite gin cocktails!

Almost Midnight

PEPPERMINT SOUTHSIDE

This cocktail doesn't make a lot of fuss because it simply doesn't need to. Although mint is actually in season in the spring and summer, it grows so abundantly that it's easy to harvest, dry, and store for use all year long. The association of peppermint with wintertime may actually just be because hard candies (often flavored with peppermint) were typically made during the colder months. Nonetheless, the cooling flavor of peppermint pairs perfectly with the lime and gin in this slight twist on the classic Southside cocktail.

- Lime wedge
- A few fresh mint leaves, plus extra for garnish
- 2 ounces gin
- 1 ounce lime juice
- 1 ounce simple syrup

1. Muddle the lime wedge with fresh mint leaves in a shaker.
2. Add ice, the gin, lime juice, and simple syrup to the shaker and shake well.
3. Strain into a coupe glass.
4. Garnish with fresh mint.

MAKE IT A MOCKTAIL

Substitute gin with club soda.

New Year's Resolutions
KALE GIN AND TONIC

Winter veggies—especially those that lend themselves to botanical cocktails—are few and far between. But year-round, almost any green vegetable gets along quite nicely with the herbal essence of gin . . . yes, even kale! Whether you're a kale aficionado or not much of a salad person yourself, give this "green juice" a shot. It's bright, effervescent, and perhaps the perfect morning-after remedy for New Year's Day.

- 3 ounces gin
- 2 ounces fresh kale juice
- ½ ounce lemon juice
- 2 ounces tonic water
- Fresh lacinato kale leaf, for garnish

1. Combine the gin, kale juice, and lemon juice in a shaker with ice and shake well.
2. Strain into a highball glass.
3. Top with tonic water.
4. Garnish with the fresh kale leaf.

MAKE IT A MOCKTAIL

Substitute gin with tonic water.

Cold Winter's Night

MAPLE JUNIPER BOURBON

Juniper berries most often find their way into botanical cocktails as the active ingredient in gin, but they're delightfully flavorful in other mixed drinks as well! In this recipe, we're pairing not just simple syrup but our old wintertime standby maple syrup with the spicy evergreen flavor of juniper. This unique combination will beautifully mellow a strong bourbon, with just a bit of club soda for a festive fizz. This decidedly botanical beverage is sure to warm you up on a cold winter's night.

- ½ ounce pure maple syrup (infused with juniper berries, if desired)
- 4 dashes ANGOSTURA® bitters or herbal bitters of your choice
- 2 ounces bourbon
- 1 ounce club soda
- Juniper berries, for garnish

1. Combine the maple syrup and bitters in a rocks glass.
2. Add the bourbon and stir.
3. Add ice and top with club soda.
4. Garnish with fresh juniper berries.

MAKE IT A MOCKTAIL

Substitute bourbon with chilled black tea.

Appendix

Recipes by Season

SPRING

As Thyme Goes By (Grapefruit Thyme Mimosa), page 43

Warrior Princess (Ginger Paloma), page 45

Bubbly Personality (Sparkling Lemonade), page 46

The Front Porch (Lavender Lemon Spritz), page 47

Love Potion No. 75 (Rose French 75), page 49

Sebastopol Mule (Rhubarb Mule), page 50

Shut Your Piehole (Strawberry-Rhubarb Daiquiri), page 51

Earth Day (Basil Mojito), page 53

The Tzatziki (Cucumber Dill Gimlet), page 54

Kentucky Prescription (Elderflower Mint Julep), page 55

The Social Butterfly (Lavender Gin Fizz), page 57

The Amelia (Vodka Aviation), page 58

Spring Sunrise (Guava Tequila Sunrise), page 59

SUMMER

Strawberry Moon Spritz (Strawberry Aperol Spritz), page 63

Tastes Like Pink Sangria (Berry Rose Sangria), page 64

Lavender Fields Forever (Lavender Blueberry Smash), page 65

Honey Bee Mine (Jasmine Elderflower Bee's Knees), page 67

Hibiscus Mojito, page 68

Savannah Nights (Peach Spritz), page 69

Kick It Up a Notch (Spicy Pineapple Margarita), page 71

Marjoram Paloma, page 73

Summer Storm Clouds (Blackberry Thyme Dark 'n Stormy), page 75

Sunset Campfire (Calendula Mezcal Mule), page 76

Sage Wisdom, page 77

Iced Dandelion Root Rum and "Coke," page 78

AUTUMN

Perfect Fall Pair (Brandied Pear Smash), page 81

The Persnickety (Persimmon Bellini), page 82

Figgy Gin and Jam, page 83

Ophelia's Legacy (Rosemary Old Fashioned), page 85

Blood Moon, page 86

Persephone's Brew (Spiced Pomegranate Whiskey Punch), page 87

Witch's Cauldron (Triple Spiced Pumpkin Punch), page 89

Listen to Your Elder (Trees) (Elderberry French 75), page 91

Autumn Spiced Cider Sangria, page 93

Apple Orchard (Triple Apple Whiskey Sipper), page 94

Smoke and Magic Mirrors (Smoky Apple Sage Margarita), page 95

Fennel Negroni, page 98

Ancestral Tribute, page 99

WINTER

Blood Orange Sidecar, page 103

Trimming the Tree (Pomegranate Martini), page 104

Brandy Orange Blossom (Orange Pomander), page 105

Cranberry Bog (Cranberry Lime Mule), page 107

Wassailing Time (Mulled Wine), page 108

Intercontinental Delight (Sumac Paloma), page 109

Hibiscus Chai Hot Toddy, page 111

Snowed In (Cardamom Oat Milk White Russian), page 112

Homemade Winter Gin, page 113

Almost Midnight (Peppermint Southside), page 115

New Year's Resolutions (Kale Gin and Tonic), page 116

Cold Winter's Night (Maple Juniper Bourbon), page 117

Recipes by Plant

ANGELICA

Homemade Winter Gin, page 113

APPLE

Autumn Spiced Cider Sangria, page 93

Apple Orchard (Triple Apple Whiskey Sipper), page 94

Smoke and Magic Mirrors (Smoky Apple Sage Margarita), page 95

Wassailing Time (Mulled Wine), page 108

BASIL

Earth Day (Basil Mojito), page 53

BLACKBERRY

Summer Storm Clouds (Blackberry Thyme Dark 'n Stormy), page 75

BLUEBERRY

Lavender Fields Forever (Lavender Blueberry Smash), page 65

BUTTERFLY PEA FLOWER

The Social Butterfly (Lavender Gin Fizz), page 57

CALENDULA

Sunset Campfire (Calendula Mezcal Mule), page 76

CARDAMOM

Persephone's Brew (Spiced Pomegranate Whiskey Punch), page 87

Witch's Cauldron (Triple Spiced Pumpkin Punch), page 89

Hibiscus Chai Hot Toddy, page 111

Snowed In (Cardamom Oat Milk White Russian), page 112

CINNAMON

Perfect Fall Pair (Brandied Pear Smash), page 81

Persephone's Brew (Spiced Pomegranate Whiskey Punch), page 87

Witch's Cauldron (Triple Spiced Pumpkin Punch), page 89

Autumn Spiced Cider Sangria, page 93

Apple Orchard (Triple Apple Whiskey Sipper), page 94

Smoke and Magic Mirrors (Smoky Apple Sage Margarita), page 95

Wassailing Time (Mulled Wine), page 108

Hibiscus Chai Hot Toddy, page 111

Homemade Winter Gin, page 113

CLOVE

Persephone's Brew (Spiced Pomegranate Whiskey Punch), page 87

Witch's Cauldron (Triple Spiced Pumpkin Punch), page 89

Autumn Spiced Cider Sangria, page 93

Apple Orchard (Triple Apple Whiskey Sipper), page 94

Wassailing Time (Mulled Wine), page 108

Hibiscus Chai Hot Toddy, page 111

CORIANDER

Homemade Winter Gin, page 113

CRANBERRY

Cranberry Bog (Cranberry Lime Mule), page 107

CUCUMBER

The Tzatziki (Cucumber Dill Gimlet), page 54

DANDELION

Iced Dandelion Root Rum and "Coke," page 78

DILL

The Tzatziki (Cucumber Dill Gimlet), page 54

ELDERBERRY

Listen to Your Elder (Trees) (Elderberry French 75), page 91

ELDERFLOWER

Kentucky Prescription (Elderflower Mint Julep), page 55

Honey Bee Mine (Jasmine Elderflower Bee's Knees), page 67

Listen to Your Elder (Trees) (Elderberry French 75), page 91

EVERGREEN

Homemade Winter Gin, page 113

FENNEL

Fennel Negroni, page 98

FIG

Figgy Gin and Jam, page 83

GINGER

Warrior Princess (Ginger Paloma), page 45

Sebastopol Mule (Rhubarb Mule), page 50

Summer Storm Clouds (Blackberry Thyme Dark 'n Stormy), page 75

Sunset Campfire (Calendula Mezcal Mule), page 76

Witch's Cauldron (Triple Spiced Pumpkin Punch), page 89

Cranberry Bog (Cranberry Lime Mule), page 107

GRAPEFRUIT

As Thyme Goes By (Grapefruit Thyme Mimosa), page 43

Warrior Princess (Ginger Paloma), page 45

Tastes Like Pink Sangria (Berry Rose Sangria), page 64

Marjoram Paloma, page 73

Intercontinental Delight (Sumac Paloma), page 109

GUAVA

Spring Sunrise (Guava Tequila Sunrise), page 59

HIBISCUS

Hibiscus Mojito, page 68

Hibiscus Chai Hot Toddy, page 111

JASMINE

Honey Bee Mine (Jasmine Elderflower Bee's Knees), page 67

JUNIPER

Homemade Winter Gin, page 113

Cold Winter's Night (Maple Juniper Bourbon), page 117

KALE

New Year's Resolutions (Kale Gin and Tonic), page 116

LAVENDER

Bubbly Personality (Sparkling Lemonade), page 46

The Front Porch (Lavender Lemon Spritz), page 47

The Social Butterfly (Lavender Gin Fizz), page 57

Lavender Fields Forever (Lavender Blueberry Smash), page 65

LEMON

Bubbly Personality (Sparkling Lemonade), page 46

The Front Porch (Lavender Lemon Spritz), page 47

The Social Butterfly (Lavender Gin Fizz), page 57

Honey Bee Mine (Jasmine Elderflower Bee's Knees), page 67

Figgy Gin and Jam, page 83

Hibiscus Chai Hot Toddy, page 111

Homemade Winter Gin, page 113

New Year's Resolutions (Kale Gin and Tonic), page 116

LIME

Warrior Princess (Ginger Paloma), page 45

Sebastopol Mule (Rhubarb Mule), page 50

Earth Day (Basil Mojito), page 53

The Tzatziki (Cucumber Dill Gimlet), page 54

Hibiscus Mojito, page 68

Kick It Up a Notch (Spicy Pineapple Margarita), page 71

Marjoram Paloma, page 73

Summer Storm Clouds (Blackberry Thyme Dark 'n Stormy), page 75

Sunset Campfire (Calendula Mezcal Mule), page 76

Smoke and Magic Mirrors (Smoky Apple Sage Margarita), page 95

Trimming the Tree (Pomegranate Martini), page 104

Cranberry Bog (Cranberry Lime Mule), page 107

Intercontinental Delight (Sumac Paloma), page 109

Almost Midnight (Peppermint Southside), page 115

MAPLE

Cold Winter's Night (Maple Juniper Bourbon), page 117

MARJORAM

Marjoram Paloma, page 73

MINT

Kentucky Prescription (Elderflower Mint Julep), page 55

Almost Midnight (Peppermint Southside), page 115

NUTMEG

Snowed In (Cardamom Oat Milk White Russian), page 112

OAT

Snowed In (Cardamom Oat Milk White Russian), page 112

ORANGE

The Persnickety (Persimmon Bellini), page 82

Ophelia's Legacy (Rosemary Old Fashioned), page 85

Blood Moon, page 86

Autumn Spiced Cider Sangria, page 93

Blood Orange Sidecar, page 103

Brandy Orange Blossom (Orange Pomander), page 105

Wassailing Time (Mulled Wine), page 108

Homemade Winter Gin, page 113

PEACH

Savannah Nights (Peach Spritz), page 69

PEAR

Perfect Fall Pair (Brandied Pear Smash), page 81

Autumn Spiced Cider Sangria, page 93

PEPPER [BLACK]

Persephone's Brew (Spiced Pomegranate Whiskey Punch), page 87

PEPPER (CHILI)

Kick It Up a Notch (Spicy Pineapple Margarita), page 71

PERSIMMON

The Persnickety (Persimmon Bellini), page 82

PINEAPPLE

Kick It Up a Notch (Spicy Pineapple Margarita), page 71

POMEGRANATE

Blood Moon, page 86

Persephone's Brew (Spiced Pomegranate Whiskey Punch), page 87

Trimming the Tree (Pomegranate Martini), page 104

Intercontinental Delight (Sumac Paloma), page 109

PUMPKIN

Witch's Cauldron (Triple Spiced Pumpkin Punch), page 89

RASPBERRY

Tastes Like Pink Sangria (Berry Rose Sangria), page 64

RHUBARB

Sebastopol Mule (Rhubarb Mule), page 50

Shut Your Piehole (Strawberry-Rhubarb Daiquiri), page 51

ROSE

Love Potion No. 75 (Rose French 75), page 49

Tastes Like Pink Sangria (Berry Rose Sangria), page 64

Blood Moon, page 86

Intercontinental Delight (Sumac Paloma), page 109

ROSE HIP

Blood Moon, page 86

ROSEMARY

Ophelia's Legacy (Rosemary Old Fashioned), page 85

Persephone's Brew (Spiced Pomegranate Whiskey Punch), page 87

SAGE

Sage Wisdom, page 77

Smoke and Magic Mirrors (Smoky Apple Sage Margarita), page 95

STAR ANISE

Witch's Cauldron (Triple Spiced Pumpkin Punch), page 89

Autumn Spiced Cider Sangria, page 93

Wassailing Time (Mulled Wine), page 108

Hibiscus Chai Hot Toddy, page 111

STRAWBERRY

Shut Your Piehole (Strawberry-Rhubarb Daiquiri), page 51

Strawberry Moon Spritz (Strawberry Aperol Spritz), page 63

Tastes Like Pink Sangria (Berry Rose Sangria), page 64

SUMAC

Intercontinental Delight (Sumac Paloma), page 109

THYME

As Thyme Goes By (Grapefruit Thyme Mimosa), page 43

Savannah Nights (Peach Spritz), page 69

Summer Storm Clouds (Blackberry Thyme Dark 'n Stormy), page 75

VIOLET

The Amelia (Vodka Aviation), page 58

Recipes by Alcohol

BRANDY

Perfect Fall Pair (Brandied Pear Smash), page 81

The Persnickety (Persimmon Bellini), page 82

Witch's Cauldron (Triple Spiced Pumpkin Punch), page 89

Autumn Spiced Cider Sangria, page 93

Blood Orange Sidecar, page 103

Brandy Orange Blossom (Orange Pomander), page 105

Wassailing Time (Mulled Wine), page 108

CIDER

Apple Orchard (Triple Apple Whiskey Sipper), page 94

GIN

Love Potion No. 75 (Rose French 75), page 49

The Tzatziki (Cucumber Dill Gimlet), page 54

The Social Butterfly (Lavender Gin Fizz), page 57

Honey Bee Mine (Jasmine Elderflower Bee's Knees), page 67

Figgy Gin and Jam, page 83

Listen to Your Elder (Trees) (Elderberry French 75), page 91

Fennel Negroni, page 98

Almost Midnight (Peppermint Southside), page 115

New Year's Resolutions (Kale Gin and Tonic), page 116

GRAND MARNIER

Trimming the Tree (Pomegranate Martini), page 104

KAHLÚA

Snowed In (Cardamom Oat Milk White Russian), page 112

RUM [DARK]

Summer Storm Clouds (Blackberry Thyme Dark 'n Stormy), page 75

Iced Dandelion Root Rum and "Coke," page 78

Blood Moon, page 86

RUM [SPICED]

Witch's Cauldron (Triple Spiced Pumpkin Punch), page 89

Brandy Orange Blossom (Orange Pomander), page 105

RUM [WHITE]

Shut Your Piehole (Strawberry-Rhubarb Daiquiri), page 51

Earth Day (Basil Mojito), page 53

Hibiscus Mojito, page 68

SCHNAPPS [PEACH]

Savannah Nights (Peach Spritz), page 69

TEQUILA OR MEZCAL

Warrior Princess (Ginger Paloma), page 45

Spring Sunrise (Guava Tequila Sunrise), page 59

Kick It Up a Notch (Spicy Pineapple Margarita), page 71

Marjoram Paloma, page 73

Sunset Campfire (Calendula Mezcal Mule), page 76

Smoke and Magic Mirrors (Smoky Apple Sage Margarita), page 95

Intercontinental Delight (Sumac Paloma), page 109

VERMOUTH

Fennel Negroni, page 98

VODKA

Sebastopol Mule (Rhubarb Mule), page 50

The Amelia (Vodka Aviation), page 58

Tastes Like Pink Sangria (Berry Rose Sangria), page 64

Lavender Fields Forever (Lavender Blueberry Smash), page 65

Trimming the Tree (Pomegranate Martini), page 104

Cranberry Bog (Cranberry Lime Mule), page 107

Snowed In (Cardamom Oat Milk White Russian), page 112

Homemade Winter Gin, page 113

WHISKEY

Kentucky Prescription (Elderflower Mint Julep), page 55

Sage Wisdom, page 77

Ophelia's Legacy (Rosemary Old Fashioned), page 85

Persephone's Brew (Spiced Pomegranate Whiskey Punch), page 87

Apple Orchard (Triple Apple Whiskey Sipper), page 94

Hibiscus Chai Hot Toddy, page 111

Cold Winter's Night (Maple Juniper Bourbon), page 117

WINE (RED)

Autumn Spiced Cider Sangria, page 93

Wassailing Time (Mulled Wine), page 108

WINE (ROSÉ)

Tastes Like Pink Sangria (Berry Rose Sangria), page 64

WINE (SPARKLING)

As Thyme Goes By (Grapefruit Thyme Mimosa), page 43

Bubbly Personality (Sparkling Lemonade), page 46

The Front Porch (Lavender Lemon Spritz), page 47

Love Potion No. 75 (Rose French 75), page 49

Strawberry Moon Spritz (Strawberry Aperol Spritz), page 63

Savannah Nights (Peach Spritz), page 69

Sage Wisdom, page 77

The Persnickety (Persimmon Bellini), page 82

Listen to Your Elder (Trees) (Elderberry French 75), page 91

Metric Conversions

(These conversions are rounded for convenience.)

Ingredient	Cups/ Tablespoons/ Teaspoons	Ounces	Grams/ Milliliters
Fruit, dried	1 cup	4 ounces	120 grams
Fruits or veggies, chopped	1 cup	5 to 7 ounces	145 to 200 grams
Fruits or veggies, puréed	1 cup	8.5 ounces	245 grams
Honey, maple syrup, or corn syrup	1 tablespoon	0.75 ounce	20 grams
Liquids: cream, milk, water, or juice	1 cup	8 fluid ounces	240 milliliters
Salt	1 teaspoon	0.2 ounce	6 grams
Spices: cinnamon, cloves, ginger, or nutmeg (ground)	1 teaspoon	0.2 ounce	5 milliliters
Sugar, brown, firmly packed	1 cup	7 ounces	200 grams
Sugar, white	1 cup/ 1 tablespoon	7 ounces / 0.5 ounce	200 grams/ 12.5 grams

Also Available

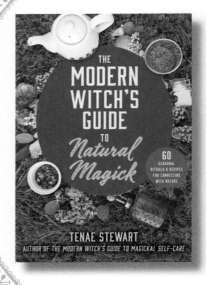